Attention Authors

5 Years Guarantee
How to make India Richer

Developmental Economics and Public Policy

Shrawan K Vikram

Manas Publications
(We Convert Fighters into Writers)
New Delhi-110002 (INDIA)

MANAS PUBLICATIONS
(Publishers, Library Suppliers, Importers & Exporters)
4402/5-A, Ansari Road
(Opp. HDFC Bank)
Darya Ganj, New Delhi-110 002 (INDIA)
Off. ✆ 23260783, 23265523, Res. ✆ 23842660
Fax: 011-23272766
E-mail: manaspublications@vsnl.com
manaspublications@gmail.com
www.manaspublications.in

ISBN 978-81-7049-384-6
Rs. 595

Typeset at
Manas Publications

Printed in India at
R K Print Services, Delhi
and published by Mrs Suman Lata for
Manas Publications, 4402/5-A, Ansari Road
(Opp. HDFC Bank),
Darya Ganj, New Delhi-110 002 (INDIA)

CONTENTS

1. Introduction 9
2. Development 15
3. What is Poverty? 20
4. Money 30
5. Resources 43
6. National Wealth 50
7. Population 59
8. Exports and Imports 65
9. Removal of Poverty 77
10. How to Remove Poverty in 5 Years? 95
11. Monetary Policy 140
12. Necessity of Standardization 161

13. Impact of Corruption 171

14. Developmental Mindsets and Attitudes 177

15. Action List—Individual Level... 186

16. Action List—Community Level... 190

17. Action List—Government Level 193

Appendices:

I. Agriculture/Food Security 205

II. Fruits and Fruit Trees 217

Index 239

I dedicate this book

to my parents

especially my father Shri Sobh Nath Lal who encouraged me to write.

to my wife Usha

who with her perseverance and comments made this work feasible.

to Readers

who will make the change to make India so prosperous as there will be no poor citizen.

Chapter - 1

INTRODUCTION

'I am born poor, but I will not die poor'

—Indian Citizen

Total removal of poverty in a short period is a matter of life and death for India. This book guides towards the process of achieving the same and ensures a richer India.

We as a nation are standing at the beginning of the 21st century, a century that will not tolerate hunger and poverty, a century during which nations will compete with each other for acquiring never achieved levels of wealth.

Therefore, it will be a century dominated by those nations with best quality of human resources imbued with initiative, with advanced technological capacity, and best infrastructure.

If India is to be an active participant in the global developments of the 21st century, we as a nation, have to quickly find ways of total removal of poverty from India. This is the first step for generating quality human resource of any nation. Advanced technological capacity and infrastructure are part of the process of total removal of poverty.

India has been independent for over 60 years now. There has not been any 5-year plan which did not talk of removal of poverty. Every political party's manifesto talks of poor and actions for uplifting the poor. But what have been the results? India still has the maximum number of poor people in any nation on this earth.

We are at a threshold today, when India as a nation, must and can do wonder by total removal of poverty in 5 years. It has not to be on paper; the concepts and approach enumerated in this book do not mention or refer to the statistics of the poor. For total removal of poverty, we don't need to count how many poor citizens we have, and subsidize items for these poor citizens. This is what present governmental set-up is doing, and it is derogatory and encroachment on human rights and dignity. The governmental setup, over the last several years, has started many schemes for urban and rural poor. These schemes like Indira Awas list, Below Poverty Line (BPL) card, Antyodaya card, etc. give privileges of obtaining subsidy on various items of necessity or receiving freebies or sometimes receiving cash by individuals or families.

These types of schemes are not helpful; rather these lead to corruption, nepotism and degeneration of politics to only distribution of freebies and not development. Whereas, development has to be the core political ethos in any nation.

Development Vision

The objective of the Developmental Economics concepts and approaches in this book is to create a Development Vision, awaken, coordinate and direct the people's efforts, minds and national resources towards highly focused seemingly impossible action plans. And if the action plans (mentioned in this book) are followed sincerely, following results are guaranteed.

- No harms done to the individuals, society and the nation; if the plans are implemented sincerely.
- All inclusive social and cultural development.
- Removal of poverty at the fastest speed feasible.

- Nation will make enormous gain in stature and wealth in the comity of nations on this globe.

First 8 chapters bring out certain fresh, out of box, a window to either a concept, or an approach, or a view which are necessary to understand the new Developmental Economics being pursued and presented in this book. Chapters 9 to 14, give the detailed activities to be pursued for total removal of poverty within 5 years. Last chapters 15, 16, 17 give macro action lists at individual level, community level, legal level and government level. The chapter on fruits and fruit trees at the end has been included, though outwardly looking out of place, because of great potential of the subject in removal of hunger and its tremendous scope in up-grading the quality of the humungous human resource this nation is blessed with.

It is recommended to read the chapters in the order presented to grasp and, to have clear understanding of the further chapters. Otherwise there is danger of missing the theme.

A few words here about the action plans will not be out of place. The action plans;

(a) are macro-level action plans. Each of the activity/target will need very detail micro-level plans and schedules.

(b) are achievable within a short period– within 5 years if systemically pursued with conviction, zeal, and all inclusive approach.

(c) are based on research, deliberation, potential and finally whether practical (sometimes also based on what other nations have done).

(d) to create a kind of enabling environment taking into account expected changes and trends in the world of tomorrow.

Determination and discipline in planning and implementation is the key to success, and is applicable to this goal too of the developmental economics. There has to be declaration of our determination to disentangle ourselves from the scourge of poverty. All sections of society – individuals, ministries and other governmental institutions, various administrative setups, private sector, public sector, educational institutions, co-operative societies, panchayats, villages, NGOs, media all will have to direct and maintain focus to contributing towards effective implementation of the activities and objectives of this Developmental Vision of 'Total Removal of Poverty in 5 Years.'

To get on the above path, it is pre-requisite that each citizen's responsibility will be to shun, eschew anything which can divide citizens on the basis of religion, region, race and gender and place of origin. Unity of nation, peace, stability and security of citizens and their property constitute a fundamental and necessary environment for development at fast speed within our democratic setup. This is not difficult since this subcontinent size nation has same cultural ethos and norms everywhere. The present day confidence level is the most conducive signal to embark on this type of programme without getting lost due to internal and external distractions.

For successful implementation of the programme, the implementation driving forces or pillars include among others, the need for a developmental attitude and mindset of innovation, creativity, and cultivation of self-reliance frame of mind. The fourteenth chapter is derived out of this need.

A development vision is an articulation of a vision which a nation envisages to attain and a plausible course of action to be taken for its achievement. A national vision of 'Removal of Poverty in 5 Years' is a mammoth vision and is feasible only by seeking to actively mobilize the people and other necessary resources (*money is not one of these*) towards the achievement of goals. The vision has to be initiated at the apex level of the nation, shared with the people to arouse people's aspirations and ignite a spark that will lift the nation to rise above the mundane.

The basic concepts presented in this book are of universal nature and will be useful for any nation and especially useful for any developing nation. However the focus is India. Examples and data are having India as a base.

Lastly, care has been exercised to present even complicated or abstract thoughts and concepts in simple language and with examples. Fear of 'Economics is not for everybody' should not deter anybody from reading this presentation; it is simple and comprehensible.

Reasons for pursuing Developmental Economics and Public Policy

Your reason for wanting to understand more on developmental economics and public policy is not important. The important thing is that you have overcome previous thought process of "nothing more is feasible" and you are ready to look afresh. You have overcome the biggest obstacle in the progress of the nation.

Perhaps you are a professor or student of Economics, or Management, or Agriculture and you wish to read and understand more on developmental economics. There is nothing wrong with this motive and this book will definitely put you on some thinking and some action mode. If that happens, the author's efforts will be of some social and academic use.

Perhaps you are or 'would-be' administrator/policy maker in the governmental setup of secretariats, research organizations, institutions, state or district administrations, defence or any wing of government, this book may be of some directional/referral value to you while making decisions. If the ideas compiled in this entity are used for uplifting the poor by your hands, it would have served its purpose.

Perhaps you are a social worker or a practising politician and this book attracted your attention since development is the most talked of subject today, you will not be disappointed on the freshness issue. At some places, it may seem to be unreasonable in its comments, but the comments only echo common citizens' sentiments and perceptions. However one thing is definite that you will opt for many of ideas as part of your organization's/party's programmes and directions to investigate and pursue. The nation will definitely be benefited.

Perhaps you are a senior politician of the ruling political party at the Centre or one of the states or one of the municipalities. You will be of opinion after reading that the government has done quite a lot and presently is implementing many of the ideas. True, but you will also realize that many of the suggestions/proposals can be implemented with different level of enthusiasm, direction and speed. If this book puts you in thinking mode of evaluation for practicability of implementing the vision; it would not have been in vain.

Perhaps you are an enlightened citizen who wants to know more about various facets of the nation's development, you will like and probably try to follow the action plan at the individual level. The nation will definitely be benefited by your pursuits.

Perhaps you are a journalist and this piece of work came to you by chance. You may feel that most of the ideas are cynic or question "who will implement?" Your push to make it happen will help the have-nots of this country.

Summary

- *Development Vision: 'Total Removal of Poverty in 5 years'.*
- *Conducive Environment is there to start the programme.*

Programme to be started now. A richer India and total poverty removal is guaranteed.

Chapter - 2

DEVELOPMENT

But no nation can base its survival and development on luck and prayers alone, while its leadership fritters away every available opportunity for success and concrete achievement.

—Ibrahim Babangida

Development word is meaningless in the context of nations and societies. What is important is wealth and its distribution to its citizens so that the citizens enjoy life free of hunger and hardship of poverty.

Some countries are called 'developed'. Some countries are called 'under-developed' and some are called 'developing'. These three words connote—'Developed' means plenty of personal, industrial and defence goods are available; 'Under-developed': shortage of personal, industrial and defence goods; 'Developing' : a word coined in 1970s to indicate that though there is some shortages or less demands for personal, industrial and defence goods, but in future it may not be so.

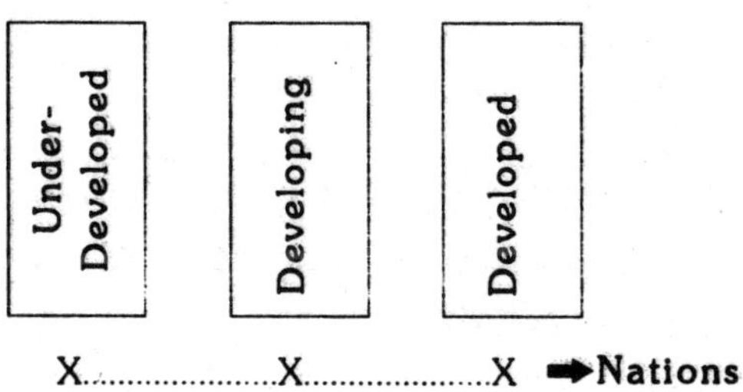

Oh No! So-called developed countries will agree only with this below.

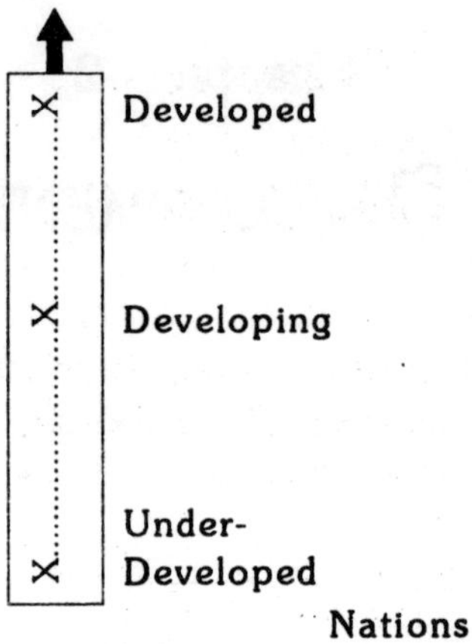

Development is just change

But the fundamental truth is that all countries in this world may be called developing because each one is doing so.

If one ponders in depth; all the above words (under-developed, developing and developed) are having hollow meaning. There is nothing as development, what we really mean is change. Some may argue that positive change is development and negative change is regression. Really, change is change; there is nothing in society as positive change or negative change.

Let us take some examples.

1. My grandfather had only two silk kurtas at any point of time. I have 20 shirts and 6 kurtas. Was my grandfather less happy than me on this account?

No, since during his period owning two silk kurtas itself comparatively was a luxury. Today in middle class owning 20 shirts and 6 kurtas is not something of great luxury.

2. Some countries i.e. USA or Russia own thousands of nuclear bombs. Most of the countries do not have even a

single nuclear bomb. Will those countries having thousands of nuclear bombs will be called developed countries and others undeveloped just because of level of possession of nuclear bombs.

3. 500 years before, an Indian farmer was in much more better position than a British farmer. Columbus and Vasco de Gama came out of their country in search of India, since India was considered a Golden Bird or much more prosperous. India had national material wealth much more than any of the European nations. Did it mean that India was more developed than any European nation? The answer would have been an emphatic NO at that time.

Just by being rich, a nation would not have been considered "Developed". At that time rather Europeans thought that their nations were more developed than India.

- 300 years before, India made very fine clothing material compared to British or any other European nation. Does it mean India was more developed? Indian fabric was hand woven whereas British fabric was mill made. The two nations made use of different technologies for the same item of use, just that.
- Today USA has more goods/services available per person compared to India. It simply means USA is richer than India. By this token alone at least USA cannot be termed more developed.

Today USA has more infrastructures (investment) per person than India. It simply means that USA has more resources (tools) per person for use than India, but it cannot be termed more developed. It is simply richer than India.

Today USA uses more technological discoveries and innovations than India, many of which might be due to hostile cold climatic conditions; it simply means that it is meeting the needs of its citizens. Just for this, USA is not more developed.

Technological changes continuously happen based on actual human needs or perceived human needs. All technological changes in the form of theories, discoveries, innovations, practices; need not necessarily be beneficial to the human society at all time to come. Chinese discovered gun powder thousands of years before Europeans but used it for entertainment purposes on special occasions. Europeans learned the same from Chinese and devised gun. Till nations were using it (gun) for winning, capturing, looting or murdering, subjugating inhabitants of other nations, it was considered good for the nation using this form of power. But when its own citizens became aware of the manufacturing processes or obtained this form of power from other sources, and started using it against their own governments/state; I don't think anybody will consider gun as development. A new term was found for such citizens as "terrorists". Of course other nations/ groups of people also started using this leverage to dominate/ subjugate, harass other nations.

A technological change of today may look beneficial and hence progressive today but may prove to be a curse in future. Similarly a technological change of today may be harmful but may be useful in future for some or all societies.

A technological change is not development, at least not a development meaning beneficial progress. Technology changes, technology level changes as societies change with time.

The German writer Johann Wolfgang von Goethe said "nature knows no pause in progress and development, and attaches her curse on all inaction". What is really true that nature has no pause in change, and attaches her curse on all inaction. As the great epic Mahabharata says that time is the most powerful and time determines the events and outcomes; whatever goes up, comes down; and changes are happening continuously in this world.

Poverty Removal is the Key

Many will claim that India has developed a lot compared to when it became independent. It has progressed in science and technology and industry. There is no point in arguing on this. Yes there has been progress.

But it is also true that there has been only marginal reduction in number of the people below poverty line. For the last few years, in real terms, there has been regression. Many of those who had improved their situation are back to their original poverty level due to excessive food inflation and general inflation. The recent galloping inflation in food items prices has thrown back a sizeable number of its citizens below so-called poverty line. Over 50% of Indian citizens are undernourished or hungry. Under these circumstances how any nation can claim any progress or development? India has got now some rich people and some middle class people. These groups have somewhat expanded recently but nobody should forget what was echoed by the Argentinean politician Evita Peron that when the rich think about the poor, they have poor ideas.

Summary

- *There is no point in talking of development and progress for a nation which has enormous number of its citizens hungry or undernourished.*
- *Total removal of poverty must be the only and sole responsibility of the political–technical plane of governance till the goal is achieved.*

India must achieve 100% poverty removal as quickly as feasible and then talk of progress and development.

Chapter - 3

What is Poverty ?

Poverty is the worst form of violence.

—M. K. Gandhi

Physical poverty in any nation is not only ugly to look at; it is a form of violence inflicted by rich on the poor. Those who are at higher pedestals of prosperity must feel dejected and they must get into soul stirring actions to eliminate the same.

Poverty is lack of food, lack of clothing or lack of shelter. That is what we understand normally and to a great extent it is true too, since food, shelter and clothing are the basic needs.

Also let us not forget that it is not necessary that all the three have to be present at the same time. A person may have good food but does not have shelter and has to sleep in the street, is definitely a poor person even if he has access to reasonable clothes.

But deciding whether a person is poor or not, is not so straight forward. Let us take a case of an individual, who is able to manage to get good clothing, has an excellent dwelling unit and also is able to manage very good quality of food i.e. grains, vegetables, milk etc. Now his son grows up and has to join higher studies. The higher studies nowadays have become so expensive that he is not able to pay the fees for the higher education of his son. If he somehow manages to pay the fees and the son's stay in hostel, then he has to sacrifice food quality, shelter quality, (some portion on rental), and also on clothes. So, though he was not poor till now, but he will slip into poverty for some period.

He has another choice, he takes loan, but whenever he has to pay back interest and capital, then he slips into poverty for much longer period, since his paying capacity is limited. If his son has to pay, he must be assured of proper employment, giving him loan repayment capability. If it does not happen, then now two individuals (actually whole family) slip into long term poverty.

This example brings a time factor to the poverty aspects, and also manifestation of poverty growth. We also cannot ignore the other living requirements and conditions like education, conveyance, electricity, water, etc., while talking of poverty.

Lack of any or all the basic three needs i.e. food, shelter and clothing is *Physical Poverty.*

Definition of Physical Poverty is Difficult

Defining physical poverty is not so straight forward. We will take some examples to see the difficulties in deciding who is poor, who is not.

- Patel lives in a village. His family owns a large tract of land in the village. He has many buffalos and cows. His family is large. Food availability to the family is plenty. He has shelter that is a village home of his family. Whatever he produces gets consumed by the family. Hence no cash generation is there and so he, his children, and other family members are seen in rags, very often in torn clothes.

Is he a poor individual?

- Agarwal is an advocate but does not have good practice. He has a big ancestral house in the city. He wears good clothes while being in the court. But when it comes to food, he or his family members cannot afford nutritious food. There is no milk purchase, hardly any vegetables, question of purchasing any fruits does not arise, and somehow he manages to buy the basic grains i.e. wheat, rice and dal. His children may be studying presently being small in age, but problems will arise when they grow up for the college education.

Is Agarwal a poor person?

- Ramakant has migrated to a city and works for a garden contractor. He has some clothes, gets food by the salary he gets from the contractor, but has no place to stay in the city, so he stays in a shanty on a public land.

Is Ramakant a poor person?

- Shanti lives in a jhoparpatti but is not short of food, clothes and has even a two-wheeler and a TV in the place.

Is Shanti a poor person?

The dilemma faced to say yes or no is indicative of multidimensional aspects of poverty. In everyday life, we sometimes come across families which were alright, reasonably well, but slipped into poverty, when a member of the family fell ill and needed costly medical attention.

So, physical poverty has gradations and various shades.

Rajeev is a student of B.A. in a city school. His school is a famous one and mostly students come from well-to-do families. Rajeev comes from a family which has food, shelter and clothing, even a two-wheeler, a small TV etc. Rajeev has many friends who come from rich families. He visits them often. He sees big houses, expensive big cars, costly furniture etc. in his friends' houses. He tells his father, mother and sister that his family is a poor family. But his father and mother do not agree to this. Parents say that they have been able to arrange everything, luxuries and necessities.

Rajeev suffers from *Psychological Poverty.*

Psychological Poverty

Do you think we should ignore Rajeev's perceptions and feelings? It may turn out to be dangerous at the formative stage of a young man.

Psychological poverty i.e. perception of being poor is worse than the physical poverty. Physical poverty keeps a person's mind busy to find out ways and means of arranging food, shelter and clothing. But in psychological poverty, the person's mind is idle and then it conspires—how to cheat the society to get the luxuries or may adapt to violent means to snatch.

A person suffering from psychological poverty, mostly thinks that the other person having all the luxuries is also just an ordinary human being–and either he unscrupulously amassed those luxuries or it is his luck. He never attributes the vast difference in the *living to great luxuries* – to the person's hard work. Also, don't you think that those who are poor and are just living, really put in much more physical and mental hard work and for longer periods during a day; than those who are having big luxuries. (Wealth word is not being used; to avoid confusion later in this book.)

As a nation something must be done to reduce the conflicts created by psychological poverty and only way will be to reduce the root cause of psychological poverty—too much difference in the resources between individuals or between families. Even in a democratic set-up, government does have manoeuvrability to control or reduce the difference so as to blunt uprisings and to control crimes in the society.

There is another class of poverty—*Social Poverty.*

Social Poverty

Social poverty is, that an individual finds himself/herself not able to perform a social function, or a ritual or any task which the person feels that it was necessary to do so for his prestige or position or status in the society/relatives or known persons due to lack of resources.

Social poverty is akin to the earlier explained psychological poverty but not the same. The newspaper article shows the social poverty and its fatal consequences sometimes.

Woman sets herself, son ablaze

TIMES NEWS NETWORK

Pune: In a shocking incident, a woman committed suicide by setting herself abiaze along with her one-year-old son because she was unable to celebrate his birthday on Thursday evening.

The Hinjewadi police have identified the deceased as Sujata Vishnu Sherkar (28), and her son as Shivam of Ranpise chawl in Bhavdan.

According to the police, Sujata was under tremendous pressure, after she found that she was not in a position to celebrate Shivam's first birthday. The couple were staying in a rented house in Bavdhan.

The police said Sujata could not make arrangements to celebrate her son's birthday as her husband was unemployed. This led her to take the drastic step

The police said that Sujata, who is a housewife, could not make alternative arrangements to celebrate the birthday because her driver husband, Vishnu, was unemployed. This led her to take the drastic step of ending her life as well as that of her son's.

According to the police, Sujata set herself and Shivam ablaze around 7 pm by pouring kerosene. Shivam died instantly due to severe degree burn injuries before he could be administered medical treatment. Sujata, who received 100 per cent burn injuries, died on Friday morning while undergoing treatment at the Sassoon general hospital. The police also said that Vishnu, who tried to douse the fire, received 20 per cent burn injuries.

After the incident came to light, police hawaldar Satyavan Thakur registered a case of culpable homicide not amounting to murder against Sujata under section 304 of the Indian Penal Code. Sub-inspector Sanjay Patil of the Hinjewadi police station is investigating the case.

The woman sets herself and son ablaze because she could not celebrate son's birthday due to lack of resources. Some people accept this gracefully, but some do not and it is a great mental stress for those who do not accept.

Psychological poverty is reducible/removable with certain actions, but the social poverty is not easy to reduce, remove or eliminate. This is due to the difference in the individuals, and even if all are rich, there will be some variations due to available resources. Also as a nation and a society become richer, the social functions go on getting added or are celebrated with an increasing pomp and show. This is due to the need of humans to differentiate from each other for the reason of self-actualization. This is due to differences in individuals, and even if all are rich, there will be some variations due to available resources on individual basis. So, over period of time, with abundance of resources, social functions go on getting added and become more ostentatious.

Take Valentine's Day celebrations in India; during and before 1970s nobody in India even knew about Valentine's Day. However when the country became economically better, Valentine's Day celebrations in the urban areas are becoming more and more popular among young Indians. It has become social event, like birthdays, marriage anniversary and other festivals. In America, there are mother's day, father's day and many other days of celebrations during the year.

In Germany (and sure in many other countries) now birthday is celebrated everyday of the month of the birth.

Hence, as prosperity increases; as affordability enhances, it gives rise to more and more partying or celebrating functions on grand scale.

In India especially urban India, marriage celebrations are more and more ostentatious.

All these create social poverty for some since some others are doing partying on a larger scale. Social poverty is less when a country's population gets only its most basic needs fulfilled. Take an example, of a village in India, in 1940s or even in 1950s, most of the village population used to live like a community. Some individuals and families may have more land and some less; but food was same, clothing was same, housings were more or less similar. Not much difference in living and hence less visible social gaps among the individuals.

But does it mean that wealth in a country should not increase? Or there should be communism. No, that is not the answer. In the villages in 1960s there were more deaths due to malnutrition and more diseases than today. Though, families may not be mingling with each other due to social poverty. Human suffering was more at that time than now– basic naked suffering has reduced dramatically in the villages.

National Poverty

National poverty is group psyche due to vast physical disparity in resources and availability of goods and services between nations. In modern day, America as a nation has amassed physical assets and resources which are at much higher level than most of the countries, and definitely India in comparison is poor.

Gross Domestic Product (GDP) or GDP based on purchasing power parity (PPP) is a good basis of comparison. Also visibility of affluence and prosperity gets compared by

GDP divided by the national population. A table below shows the difference between India and some of the developed nations.

Purchasing Power Parity is estimated based on the prices of goods in various countries. Exchange rate between currencies is estimated based on such data. This exchange rate for US dollar to rupee is approximately one fourth of the official rate. That is rupee is approximately four times stronger than what is projected by the official rate.

Table 1: GDP Comparison*

Country	India	UK	Japan	Germany	USA
GDP* (based on PPP) US$ trillions	3.3	2.2	4.3	2.9	14.3
GDP* comparison (India as base)	100	68	133	88	437
GDP* / Citizen US$	2800	36600	34200	34800	47000
GDP*/Citizen Comparison (India as base)	100	1307	1221	1242	1679

The above table gives flash of blinding light:

1. GDP* based on PPP shows the earnings of the nation (wealth produced every year monetized on common base.). UK a small island has earnings per year 68% of India, Japan a small island has 33% higher annual earnings than India, Germany a country equivalent to one of the states in India has earnings 88% of India and US having population 1/3rd of India has yearly earnings over four times. It is sad but true.

*GDP is Gross Domestic Product (GDP) based on Purchasing Power Parity (PPP).

2. GDP*/Citizen Comparison are still more glaring. It shows how poor we Indians are. If an Indian earns/uses goods and services worth Rs. 100 per year (just for comparison sake), a British earns Rs. 1307, a Japanese Rs. 1221, a German Rs. 1242 and an American Rs. 1679.

National Poverty for India—Bad Scenario

In India everybody will say that we know that they are rich. But the table shows how glaringly they are rich and how much ground has to be covered.

The above comparison is done on Purchasing Power Parity (PPP) basis and not on the official currency exchange rates. If the comparison is made on the basis of official exchange rate for dollars or pounds, the scenario will be many times worse than shown above. But then it will not be real scenario because of excessive distortion in the official currency exchange rates for the currencies of the developed nations to Indian currency.

The parliamentarians may say anything but action is too slow and understanding of the problem is dismal at national and state level.

To overcome this situation petty politics has to be given up and concentrated endeavor by central Government, State Governments and every citizen is required. All have to work towards the catch up work to remove real physical poverty, destitution, psychological, social and national poverty.

Poverty is a relative status. If all were destitute, individuals will not feel, but if some are filthy rich and other destitute, the destitute will feel bad everyday and actions may be positive or negative. Let us work on positives because that makes citizens' life with fewer hardships. The negative path will bring only hardship to citizens.

In such a dismal scenario the people of the poorer nation start thinking inferior to the people of the rich nation. And people of the rich nation think and behave superior to the people of the poor nations.

In old days India was rich by comparison and Indians started thinking that they are superior creation than other races like whites and blacks. They even coined a word for foreigners 'mlesksha' with meaning of being dirty and untouchable.

In the 19th century whites started thinking as a superior race compared to brown, yellow and black races. This was propagated by some individuals and it was consequence of the war resources mastered by them. Some individuals published papers and literatures showing scientific corroborations. They started propagating that IQ of the white race individual happens to be more and that is why they are more prosperous. In essence it was similar to historical Indian thinking of superiority as a race or as a nation.

But in reality, all human beings of different races and of various nations are similar for all practical purposes, just like apes have different races, monkeys have different looking features in different forests.

India is a good example for monkeys. Monkeys of north India look brown and red, and of bigger size, monkeys of south India have blackish white colour of skin with black face and long tail, monkeys of north-east India are small and have yellow skin and face. And monkeys of mid India have a mixture of all this and also all the varieties. Has any monkey race right to call itself superior to other monkey race? Indian culture made some of the individual monkeys great personalities but never a monkey sub-race. Hanuman, Bali and Sugriv belonged to monkey race but their monkey sub-race was never enumerated or glorified. Similarly, human race may have many sub-races but all are humans and with similar biological traits.

A nation's prosperity or high flow in resources is dependent on time. The ups and downs are phases in history. And there may be many reasons for prosperity or poverty.

Globalization is really increasing the gap between prosperous and poor nations. Globalization is giving more military and economic powers in the hands of those who already have better resources, and also growth in military and economic powers of these countries is at much higher rate in absolute value terms because these developed countries are able to harness ideas and technologies from all over the world.

On national level, the change may sometimes be abrupt—both ways i.e. suddenly becoming prosperous or becoming poor all of a sudden. Example oil resources made many countries very rich very quickly. War or natural calamity has made many countries very poor in a short span of time in history.

Summary

- *Physical poverty is that some citizens are not able to feed themselves properly or clothe themselves properly or do not have shelter.*
- *Also all citizens of a nation must be able to have their basic needs fulfilled and goods and services for this purpose should be available to one and all.*
- *100% removal of physical poverty will also reduce 'psychological poverty', 'social poverty' and 'national poverty'. This means all inclusive poverty removal is neccessary.*

India has over 50% of its citizens below subsistence level, though really all citizens should have been wealthy, well fed, well clothed and with decent accommodation. It is the worst form of violence, bad governance unleashes on majority of its citizens.

All citizens need to do something on topmost priority basis.

Chapter - 4

MONEY

Only when the last tree has been cut down;
Only when the last river has been poisoned;
Only when the last fish has been caught;
Only then will you find out that money cannot be eaten.

—Proverb, American Indian

Money is not wealth;
money is not resource;
money is an instrument of exchange for distribution of goods and services to the citizens of a country.

All of us think that money is not available to do certain developments or to do at the pace desired. If school wants to have a building, it needs money to construct the building. It is very true at the micro level or at individuals level or even at organizational level.

But is it true at the national level?

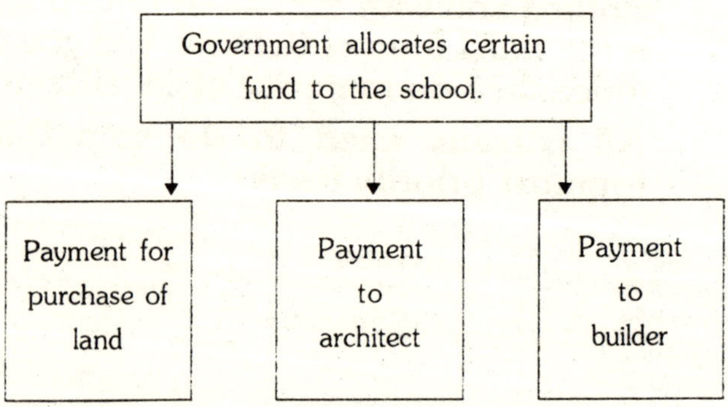

Let us look at the national level. If the government wants to have a building, it has to allocate funds to the school to have the building; to pay for land, to the architect, and builder, and so on.

But then who is printing the notes to be allocated as fund, Government itself. These are printed papers (with certain legal promises in essence) using which the land seller, architect and the builder either will buy certain goods, or make payments to other service providers or save.

Money is not National Wealth

Money in itself is not wealth. The Government has not created wealth for the nation by printing notes or minting coins. Government has just created a method to distribute or exchange goods and services as enumerated below. When the school building will get built, that will be the wealth and that will be created by people involved in building; and by using certain other resources (goods) besides their own mental and physical labour.

Coming back to our example:

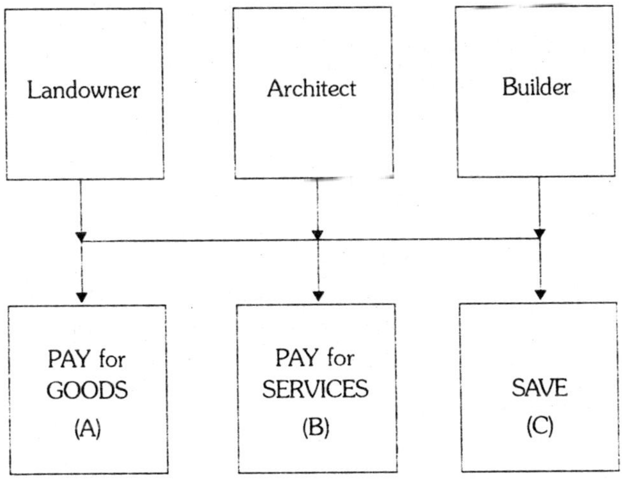

Net effect for the land seller, architect and builder is that each one of these three can afford (or society has arranged) nutritious food, good clothing and good housing. Also they can afford certain other goods like vehicle, TV, washing machine etc. Hence it will not be out of place that they got gainfully employed or the net effect on these three is same as they were employed in good salaried jobs.

Money circulates to get necessities by Citizens

Now let us evaluate the next three categories.

A. Those who got payments for providing goods to the land seller, architect and the builder.

B. Those who got payments for providing services to the land seller, architect and the builder.

C. Savings of the land seller, architect and the builder.

A. Those who got payments for providing goods to the landowner, architect and the builder.

Net effect to these people (though in business) is that each one of these can afford (actually society has arranged) food, clothing and housing plus some essential goods and some non essential goods. Really, these people got gainfully employed (same as in employment).

Also, let us not forget that many of these individuals again pay for goods, and/or for services, and/or save.

Hence, money has worked as means of distribution of goods by the society/nation.

B. Those who got payments for providing services to the land Seller, Architect and the Builder: These individuals also got gainfully employed and may have employed more individuals during the work.

In case of services too, money has worked as means of getting services offered by the society.

C. Saving could be of two types.

(i) Either put in bank or bonds or shares or any other form of financial instruments: This circulates as fund and treatment may be given as in the starting of this chapter i.e. ultimately allocation of the fund for some activity.

This money will get into circulation for distribution of goods and services or saving.

(ii) Dead saving is that one keeps the printed notes. This, in "present period of time, is a notional money and of no use; though in future" it may become live to be used for purpose A and B or C (i).

The above example illustrates that if persons have to be provided with food, clothing, housing and other goods, they have to be gainfully employed unless given in charity. Money serves well the purpose of exchange or distribution of goods and services. As Francis Bacon said 'money is like muck, not good except it to be spread'.

Since, we do not want to give any item (including money) in charity, and also since people do not like receiving in charity at society or national level, *employment becomes the basic requirement for providing food, clothing, housing and other goods.*

But, then do we have the colossal money required for giving employment to everybody?

Let us reframe this question. On the macro–level i.e. as a nation do we really need money to provide employment, in turn to provide food, clothing, housing and other goods?

Employment and Compensation

As a nation; if we decide to provide food, clothing, housing and other goods, we must gainfully employ every able bodied male/female in the working age, but there are three alternatives to compensate as given below.

(a) Need not pay money for all his needs, pay in terms of goods and/or services. (Example could be of free living-in accommodation with food and clothes and transport to wok place.)

Or (b) Partially pay in the form of goods and/or services and some paper money. (Example could be of medical hospital facility provided by some organizations or of club facility)

Or (c) Pay only in the form of paper money.

Total paper money to be printed is based on prices for goods and services required for the total population. Ideally this will be balanced if the goods and services produced on national scale match the total need of the population.

Preference may be for (b) to start with the programme.

Essential and Non-essential Goods and Services in National Planning Process

Let us take a small model of group of 5 persons named Ramesh (P1), Raghunath (P2), Seethalaxmi (P3), Madhuri (P4), and Hema (P5).

Items required annually/person

	Ramesh **P1**	*Raghu* **P2**	*Seetha* **P3**	*Madhuri* **P4**	*Hema* **P5**
Food	F 1	F2	F3	F4	F5
Clothing	C1	C2	C3	C4	C5
Housing	H1	H2	H3	H4	H5
Other Goods	G1	G2	G3	G4	G5

In a democracy each individual's choice or preference has to be taken care of. That is the real difference between democracy and communism. To meet individual needs and also choices, each one of the requirements is broken down again adding prefix 'e' for essential and 'c' for favourites (choices/preferences).

Items required annually/person

	Ramesh P1	*Raghu* P2	*Seetha* P3	*Maduri* P4	*Hema* P5
Food	eF1	eF2	eF3	eF4	eF5
	+cF1	+cF2	+cF3	+cF4	+cF5
Clothing	eC1	eC2	eC3	eC4	eC5
	+cC1	+cC2	+cC3	+cC4	+cC5
Housing	eH1	eH2	eH3	eH4	eH5
	+cH1	+cH2	+cH3	+cH4	+cH5
Other	eG1	eG2	eG3	eG4	eG5
Goods	+cG1	+cG2	+cG3	+cG4	+cG5

Total Essential = eF1+eC1+eH1+eG1+eF2+eC2+eH2+eG2+eH1+eH2 +eH3+eH4+eH5+eG1+eG2+eG3+eG4+eG5 = E

Though 'e' is shown as one value, but actually it will be a variable. Food may have e=0.9 whereas clothing may have e=0.7 and other goods e=0.5. Similarly (c) is also variable.

		Food	*Clothing*	*Housing*	*Other Goods*
Example 1:					
	e	0.9	0.7	0.8	0.5
	c	0.1	0.3	0.2	0.5
Or					
Example 2:					
	e	0.7	0.7	0.7	0.7
	c	0.3	0.3	0.3	0.3
Or					
Example 3:					
	e	0.6	0.3	0.5	0.9
	c	0.4	0.7	0.5	0.1

Or

Example 4:

e	0.5	0.5	0.5	0.5
c	0.5	0.5	0.5	0.5

Or

Example 5:

e	0.3	0.3	0.3	0.3
c	0.7	0.7	0.7	0.7

Just to understand, example 4 is chosen for explanation i.e. of all requirements of the 5 individuals 50% of the requirements will be made common and 50% of the requirements will be per individual choice.

Let us try to understand what the above means in reality.

Food: Annual requirements (value chosen here are arbitrary and for concept understanding only.)

Essentials:

	Ramesh	*Raghu*	*Seetha*	*Madhuri*	*Hema*	
	P1	**P2**	**P3**	**P4**	**P5**	**Total**
Rice (Kg.)	50	50	50	50	50	250
Wheat (Kg.)	50	50	50	50	50	250
Toor Dal (Kg.)	20	20	20	20	20	100
Chana Dal (Kg.)	10	10	10	10	10	50
Moong Dal (Kg.)	10	10	10	10	10	50
Urad Dal (Kg.)	10	10	10	10	10	50
Potatoes (Kg.)	40	40	40	40	40	200
Lemon	100	100	100	100	100	500

Lauki (kg.)	50	50	50	50	50	250
Milk (liter)	100	100	100	100	100	500
Butter (kg.)	4	4	4	4	4	20
Cabbage (kg.)	50	50	50	50	50	250

This is with assumption that the above will keep the persons in sustaining health at minimum level. There are no fruits added to the above list, no variety of vegetables added, also other items required in the kitchen for preparing food have not been included. The above is an example for understanding only.

Similarly further:

Favourite Food Items: (Choices/Preferences)

	Ramesh **P1**	*Raghu* **P2**	*Seetha* **P3**	*Madhuri* **P4**	*Hema* **P5**	**Total**
Rice (Kg.)	10	50	20	0	30	110
Wheat (Kg.)	60	0	30	70	10	170
Meat (Kg.)	0	0	0	50	10	60
Vegetable (Kg.)	100	70	60	30	90	350
Fruits (Kg.)	50	50	10	30	40	180
Eggs (nos.)	0	360	150	70	200	780

The group requirement of essential items—rice 250 kg., wheat 250kg., toor dal 100kg., chana dal 50kg., moong dal

50 kg., urad dal 50 kg., potatoes 200 kg., 500 lemons, lauki 250 kg., milk 500 liter, butter 20 kg. and cabbage 250 kg. must be produced or arranged to sustain living.

The essential items must be produced and distributed to the five individuals because it is required to maintain proper living and health, irrespective of whether they work, study, play, maintain house or do nothing. The same becomes truly applicable for all citizens of a nation but on much larger scale. It may include some services too besides goods.

The above example also shows how the planning process has to start at the national level for essential and choice items. Availability and distribution of essential items to fulfill basic needs of human beings is removal of poverty in a nation.

Distribution of Essentials

Now for distribution of essentials: it may be distributed to the five individuals with some records of distribution or without any record or against partial payment towards work or against money. Whatever system is adopted it must be ensured that all the five get it irrespective of any visible contribution to the society in general. The individual is entitled for their essential items just because he is a member of the group; the individual is a member of a nation if example is extended to the national level.

Many will object to this seemingly free distribution or some will say it is subsidy. But this argument is irrelevant. Consider that Ramesh is a working adult, Raghunath is Ramesh's old father, Seetalaxmi is Ramesh's old mother, Madhuri is wife, and Hema is the girl child of Ramesh and Madhuri. In such a case, does Ramesh say that he is feeding father, mother, wife, and child for free and subsidy is being given to the parents, wife and the child? Definitely his answer will be categorical NO. Ramesh will say that father, mother, wife and child are members of the family and he is earning for these also. Plus it is his duty to maintain the family.

If the same logic is extended to the nation, every member of the nation has right to essentials and it is national obligation and not a subsidy for those who are not contributing by work. As per Maslow's hierarchy of needs food, clothing and shelter are at the bottom of the pyramid in physiological needs and must be satisfied for all the citizens.

Maslow's Hierarchy of Needs

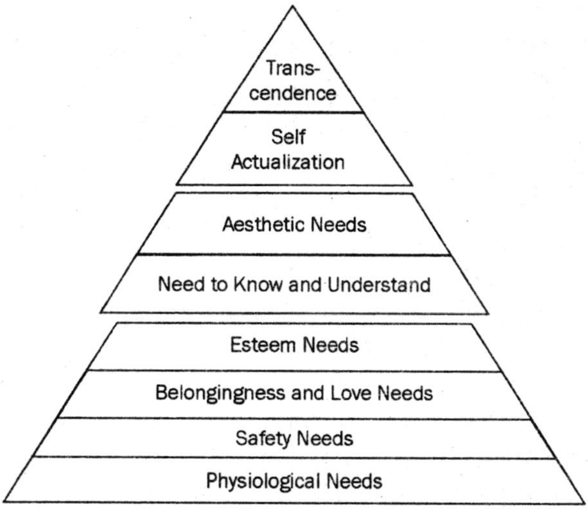

It may be appropriate here to start a norm. The word **subsidy** is never to be used in connection of fulfilling the basic needs of a nation's citizens. Whatever is done to feed, clothe and provide shelter to citizens is part of governance and if any monetary help is provided that must be called '**citizen fund**'. If a government gives monetary help to farmers on fertilizers, it is not subsidy; it is '**citizen fund**'. But if monetary help is given on petrol for cars, it is subsidy since it is satisfying higher level need and not basic or physiological need.

Hence, talk of money is irrelevant as far as distribution of essential foods or essential goods are concerned.

Free Market Mechanism for Non-essentials

Now let us move to the individual choices of items. Giving choice is democracy.

If we have to keep the order in the group of the 5 individuals, it is necessary to satisfy the individuals so that they eat what they want to eat, then the group will remain as a cohesive group for much longer period. This is the democracy for the group of the 5 individuals.

Hence, the favourite (choice or preference) food items also must be produced and distributed. For distribution of favourite food items:

(a) There has to be a barter system or instrument for distribution and money serves the purpose.

(b) An element of motivation to work at higher level intellectually and physically may be introduced. However, it does not mean that only working men or women get these, since these items are being produced for all the five; five must get these and consume otherwise it will go waste. But it may be necessary to introduce an element of competition and pricing and availability of money to individuals in such a fashion that higher quantity of favourite items will demand a little extra effort.

Let us go to another aspect. Let us assume that we have produced food for each individual of the group of 5 and the favourite food items have to be distributed using money as the instrument of exchange.

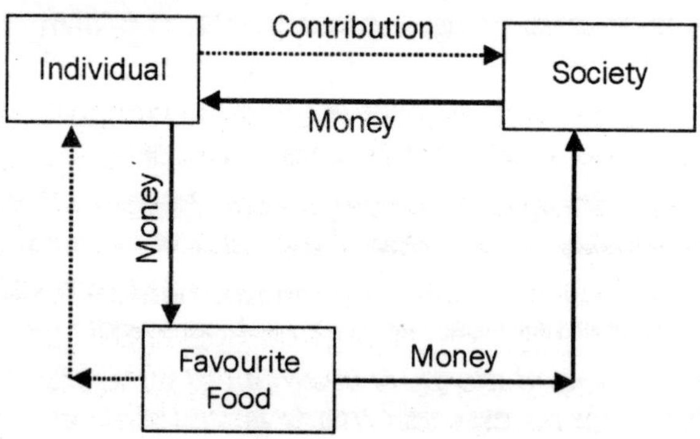

From above, we may device a system that more contribution to society means more money and in turn availability of more quantity of "favourite food".

Since society is giving money to the individual and later receiving the same money, amount of money it prints will get determined by the pricing of the 'favourite food'. The money supply and the quantity of 'favourite food items' production will get balanced by free market pricing mechanism.

How will it happen? Let us go to example. We are discussing only food to be received/bought by Ramesh. If Ramesh gets more money for his contribution to society and he needs less 'favorite food items'; and if he has nothing else to procure, more money will be of no use to him in the long range. Hence, he will not mind paying more for the 'favourite food item' for the lesser quantity or the same quantity. Price will rise till it balances.

If he gets less money and is not able to buy the 'favourite food', some quantity of favourite food will get wasted since it is already produced for him. Price of the 'favorite food' will go down to avoid the partial wastage.

Of course all these happen if the conditions were ideal; this is free market mechanism.

Exactly same analysis could be done for the 'clothing', 'housing', and 'other goods'.

Summary

- *Money is not national wealth.*
- *Money in itself is not goods or services needed by people.*
- *Money is an instrument of exchange or distribution of goods and services to the people.*
- *Wealth in a nation is created by people by making goods or by providing services.*
- *Since money is an instrument of exchange or distribution of goods and services; its management is important, otherwise it will affect the distribution of goods and services to all people.*
- *Distribution is to happen differently of 'essential' and 'choice' goods and services in a democratic setup.*

- *For essential items aim should be to let all the citizens get the same.*
- *Free Market Mechanism to apply for non-essential goods and services.*

Since money in itself is not goods or services—in principle, its availability is no issue at National Level for removal of poverty. But, money management plays a major role in distribution of goods and services to the people and consequently bad money management may lead to some people remaining poor.

Chapter - 5

RESOURCES

Pollution is nothing but the resources we are not harvesting. We allow them to disperse because we have been ignorant of their value.

—R. Buckminister Fuller

The natural resources are the available quantity of basic elements (117 of Periodic Table of elements) on the earth and humans do not have powers to add or subtract to the same in any substantial quantity.

"Despite impressive gains in economic investment and output, India faces pressing problems such as significant overpopulation, environmental degradation, extensive poverty, and widespread corruption."

That is a quote from web site of CIA of United States of America from internet www.cia.gov./library/publications/theworldfactbook/geos/IN.htm

If we talk about removal of poverty or only poverty we always quote 'scarcity of resources', 'rising population', 'resources getting distributed over too much of population' etc. etc.

A. If we are talking about earth's resources and earth's population, the above is true undoubtedly. However, its impact is inconsequential on earth. The planet will survive.

Hundred years before air was used by one billion humans and now the same air is being used by 6 billion humans. But total number of living individuals on earth i.e. all plants, all insects, all animals is too large; all use air and in this context then change of 1 billion to 6 billions is /may be a microscopic change. Same is true for all life giving elements or substances which form as resource on earth.

Next item is mined resources of earth. These are minerals, water and what else we think of and these are being mined or harnessed at great speed and converted to other substances or refined for further use. Nature has placed certain elements and compounds in localized forms and in somewhat concentrated forms. Uranium and gold are the best examples. We are depleting these types of resources undoubtedly and as human population increases greater and greater pressures occur naturally on these resources.

But there is another shade to the above story and without that the story is not complete.

Scientifically atoms do not breakup that easily and those which breakup is too few in numbers compared to the total number of atoms on this earth. Man has been able to breakup some atoms in laboratory, but how many?

Otherwise quantities of atoms of basic elements remain same in nature. It may combine to form molecules i.e. various types of compounds or substances, Nature does produce atoms of various types (of elements) using subatomic particles, but the process is at speed at other places than on earth. It is happening on sun at rapid speed. On/in earth, this process is so slow that for all practical purposes one may ignore this type of chemical reaction and safely conclude that number of atoms of any particular element remains constant on earth for very long periods of time (let us say over 1000 years).

A few examples will explain. Man is mining iron at greater and greater speed and converting it to different forms. But number of iron atoms (Fe) remain same in earth's domain. Except; earlier most of these atoms were inside the earth and now increasingly on earth after mining of iron ore. Same is true for Gold or Aluminium or Water.

Oil (diesel/petrol) is mixture of certain hydrocarbons found mainly inside the earth. Hydrocarbons are compounds of hydrogen and carbon, when it is burnt carbon combines with atmospheric gases to produce other gases and hydrogen forms some other compounds. But quantities of hydrogen(H) and carbon(C) as elements are not destroyed.

Hence, moral of this story is that man really cannot deplete or destroy the resources on/of earth. Man may be changing the look or form or making new compounds but total quantity of basic elements (117 as per Periodic Table of elements) on planet earth remains same. Man may be changing the availability pattern but definitely not the availability.

As advancement in science happens, many of the substance forming processes found in nature are becoming reversible or duplicated in laboratories and factories too. Example, today diamond is produced in laboratories and factories. What humans do, nature also does. What nature does, mankind also is learning to do the same.

A time may come, that mankind has extracted all the iron (Fe) from the earth and no more left inside the earth. But this cannot be given undue worry, since mankind will find out alternate substitute material in future or will find out process to collect back all the iron which is not in use, so as to use the same to form new items required. Same will be true for gold, aluminium, oil etc. For oil either alternate energy sources will be developed or a reversible process will be invented to make oil inside factories.

Destruction should really be termed as change in context of nature. One and all, everything, must change over a period of time, time period may be very high or low.

Let us take example of ant as specie. I am sure total number of ants on this earth must be many thousands of billions i.e. many trillions. Ants move earth, make mounds, destroy trees, structures etc. If some ants could speak and tell that they are destroying resources at a great scale and that will be harmful to ants, no ant will listen. If we listen to this statement spoken by ants, we will only laugh at those ants saying this. Actually, some will argue that ants are doing benevolent job i.e. they change earth surface, tree fall and rot, and these are essential processes in a forest to renew forest.

Similar way, we should view changes being affected by humans, also as a process of change in nature.

At last it is said to drive home, that we cannot, we do not have power yet, to affect depletion of natural resources (basic elements) on this mother earth to any great extent. We may transform the natural resources from one state to another but there is no repeat no reduction of the natural resources.

So, when one has to vanish poverty, don't let the focus get distracted by statements of overpopulation, environmental degradation etc. We as humans yet do not have powers to destroy basic elements on this planet earth. Rest all is reversible.

B. Other resources? To create wealth; there are only three ways to create wealth. First; what you grow on earth's surface. Second; what you mine or take from within or from the atmosphere of the earth. Third; what we produce using earth's resources and our mental and physical power. Fourth method may get added if we start mining on other astronomical bodies in heaven like moon or mars but that is in future.

First method: agriculture/forestry is wealth creation since food sustains us.

Second and third methods are complimentary to each other. A nation's natural resources are what minerals are found in that nation and its population.

Population of a nation is not a curse, it is its resource. *If population is properly harnessed, it will create wealth for itself.*

As a nation we have pretty good natural resources.

A comparative table of a few relevant resources highlights the same.

Table 2: Resource Comparison

Resource	*India*	*UK*	*Japan*	*Germany*	*USA*
• Area (sq. Km.) x 32876	100	7	11	11	299
• Land (sq. Km.) x 29732	100	8	13	12	308
• Arable Land (sq. Km.) x 14518	100	4	3	8	114
• Irrigated Land (sq. Km.) x 5580	100	0.3	4.6	0.9	40
• Population *(million)*	1166	61	127	82	307
• Population Density on Irrigated Land (Persons/sq. Km.)	2089	35949	4902	16975	1372
Population Density on irrigated land% (India as base)	**100**	**1720**	**235**	**813**	**66**

India has arable land which is very high. Irrigated land for agriculture is very very high, even USA is having only 40% of India's irrigated land area.

Population is a resource and again India is excellently endowed. Overpopulated are UK, Japan and Germany, rather badly overpopulated when we look at the population per square km. of irrigated land. It is unbelievable that UK has 17 times more population per square km. of irrigated land compared to India. Think of the food pressure on UK as a nation and the food poverty that country should suffer. Similarly Japan and Germany should suffer food poverty and these are the countries which need to control their population and not India. Only USA is in somewhat better condition.

For most of the resources, if similar relevant comparisons are made, India is much better placed than most of those so-called developed nations.

- India ranks first in world in availability of irrigated land.
- India ranks second in world for reserves of manganese.
- India ranks second in world in availability of manpower for military services, next to China.
- India ranks third in world in availability of water area next to Canada and USA.
- India ranks third in world for reserves of chromium.
- India ranks fourth in world for reserves of bauxite.
- India ranks fifth in world for reserves of good quality iron ore.

Of the 89 minerals produced in India, 4 are fuel minerals, 11 metallic, 52 non-metallic, and 22 minor minerals.

Let us take stainless steel which is produced using iron, manganese and chromium. India produces and also has reserves of these metals. But if one goes to USA or Europe, all public use items are made of stainless steel. Whereas, all public use items in India are made of just ordinary steel or cast iron – aesthetically looking bad and also of much less life due to rusting.

A few more examples:

- India is number 1 in world for production of tea.
- India is number 1 in world for production of milk.

- India is number 1 in world for production of pulses.
- India is number 2 in world for production of sugarcane.
- India is number 2 in world for production of wheat.
- India is number 2 in world for production of paddy.
- India is number 2 in world for production of fruits.

With above, actually this country India should be wealthy and not poor. Its people should be rich and not poor or hungry.

Summary

- *Mankind cannot destroy natural resources, humans only change the form. So no reason to get distracted.*
- *High population of a nation is not a curse, it is its resource.*
- *India has pretty good resources; its citizens should be rich.*

India has abundant resources needed for alleviation of poverty. Only it should not be frittered away by exports.

Chapter - 6

NATIONAL WEALTH

Kautilya holds that wealth and wealth alone is important, inasmuch as charity and desire depend upon wealth for their realization.

—*Arthashastra* by Kautilya, Book II, The Duties of Government Superintendents,
Chapter XXXIV– The Superintendent of Passport.

Every nation having ambitions has to pass through this century with the weapon of wealth. What this century worships is wealth. The god of this century is wealth. To succeed one must have wealth. At all cost one must have wealth.

Whether we consider a nation or a person, wealth is an abundance of valuable resources or material possessions. The concept of wealth is of great importance in economics, especially developmental economics. The meaning of wealth is not straight forward. There are so many concepts and definitions by different authors with reference to the various contexts.

Some definitions of wealth are quoted below.

"We call wealth everything whose value is measured by money."

-Aristotle (384 BC–322 BC)

"All wealth is product of Labour"
–John Locke (1632-1704)
The Wealth of Nations (1776)

"Wealth is annual produce of land and labour of the society."
–Adam Smith

"Everything forms therefore a part of Wealth which has power of purchasing."
–John Stuart Mill (1806-1873)

"Real wealth was derived from the use of energy to transform materials into physical goods and services."
–George Allen and Unwin
Wealth, Virtual Wealth and Debt (1926)

With reference to business, definition of national wealth is the value of assets minus liabilities to foreign nations or individuals at a point in time. This should include human capital too. Some economists do not include human capital due to its nature of being intangible. But then at national level, there are so many assets which are not tangible.

Max Weber's (1864–1920) concept of wealth of a nation connected to religion and beliefs is not correct application to India and is misguiding. He was not aware or ignored some major inputs or was racially biased. His two papers (considered seminal) 'The Protestant Ethic and the Spirit of Capitalism' and 'The religion of India; The Sociology of Hinduism and Buddhism' were widely circulated and at that time many of our political pundits and economists started agreeing with the view. His logic to connect Hindu religion for not being helpful in producing material wealth is erroneous. First, during his time period (1864-1920) India was under foreign rule. He did not consider the process of wealth creation in one nation by looting of another nation adapting direct aggression or subtle exploitation or combination of the two for a long period.

He also missed or ignored one basic historical fact that India's and Indian Citizens' wealth was highest in the world (including of those Christian and Protestant countries) in the previous many many centuries. India was symbolized as 'Golden Bird' by the same Christian and Protestant countries. The Europeans found ('discovered' word is politically incorrect in present day) new lands while searching for sea routes to India. Many historians attribute India's trade surplus as cause for the fall of Roman Empire.

The word wealth is often confused with income. The two terms mean differently though somewhat related. Wealth is what assets are owned by a nation, whereas income of a nation is the quantum of inflow of money. If there is large expenditure, the wealth may become negative even though there may be large income.

However to conclude, national wealth is resources and infrastructure and minerals and goods owned by the nation or citizens; and its human capital. Wealth potential of a nation is equally important as harnessing of the same at the earliest makes more citizens wealthier if distributed properly; and lower the number of the citizens of the nation at that time and of many future generations not to go through the hardship of poverty.

Methods of Creation of Wealth

There are only 4 methods of creation of wealth for nations. As it has been explained in the previous chapter of 'Money'; money is not wealth of a nation.

(a) Extraction/use of what is found/grown on earth surface.

Examples: various gems, rivers, lakes, ponds, seacoasts, mountains, forests, animals, trees, vegetation, land, agricultural produce, human capital_ _ _.

(b) Mining below and on or above earth's surface.

Examples: minerals like gold, iron, manganese, silver, chromium, uranium, thorium, mica, coal, oil, _ _ _; gases like natural gas, nitrogen, oxygen, hydrogen _ _ _ ; salts, water _.

(c) Production

Examples: all manufactured goods—earthmoving vehicles, trucks, buses, missiles, tanks, cars, TVs, washing machines, aero planes, _ _ _ ; all built items – buildings, houses, schools, offices, factories, railways, airports, stadiums,_ _ _; all arts and crafts items- carvings, paintings, films, music, _ _ _.

(d) Loot /Exploitation

Examples: Some of the European nations and most of the present day developed nations adapted this on large scale in the last few centuries. But it is not recommended on ethical and moral grounds; and in all probability a prophecy, of its being short lived in history may come true. Rather it may engulf the whole human population to a disastrous conclusion.

All the above 4 methods depend on the technological levels of the nation, how well are its people employed, earlier created wealth and lastly wealth collected by looting or exploiting another nation.

The other type of wealth i.e. spiritual wealth is acquired by society out of living experiences and does change with time or at least changes its colour and facets with time. The aim of this book is not removal of spiritual property and hence we leave this aspect here only.

Human nature revels in possession of material wealth, some essential and some non-essential.

Essential wealth items of a nation are basic to survival like food, clothing and shelter. Every human society must strive to provide these essentials to every member. If any member does not get these, he or she is poor. Poor is a relative word and this member is poorer compared to many of the members of the same society.

Non–essential wealth items are those which satisfy certain psychological need or physical need i.e. entertainment, comfort, convenience etc. A TV is not an essential wealth in a household but it does satisfy some psychological and/or physical needs. Non–essential wealth items are highly technologically evolved or rarely found and are introduced in the market after a need is created or need exists in dormant form.

If a man has not got a TV, we may or may not call him poor. In a poor country, not having a TV is not seen as a part of poverty whereas in a rich country not having a TV may be viewed by some other members of that country as part of poverty.

Hence, the view is of genre nature. To understand let us take a chimpanzees group in the forest. In this forest, for this group of chimpanzees, each member has its basic needs fulfilled and also enjoys a certain degree of freedom i.e. it eats what it likes and sleeps when and where it wishes. If any member of the group is not able to eat or sleep, what and when it wished, it is either a sick chimpanzee (may not survive long) or a weak chimpanzee and out of sympathy we will call that member a "poor chimpanzee".

Let us go to human societies. If an item is possessed by one member, and if it is feasible to duplicate enough numbers, then all members of a society (nation) must be entitled to possess one of that unless any specific member is not interested. We may not be able to achieve this 100%, but we must strive for this achievement to make meaning of society worthwhile.

This ideology makes it necessary to produce ample volumes of any comfort or convenience item and equitable distribution to members is even more important. It may be communist ideology of Karl Marx, how does it matter? It is not to undermine the doctrine of free economic market of Adam Smith as described in his book 'Wealth of Nations'.

But next goal is definitely not out of communist philosophy. Each man also must have freedom to own, or own a possible variant or altogether different item as a substitute. Individual must have the freedom of choice and taste.

And it is possible to satisfy both of the above if not 100%, very close to this target. Both of the above paragraphs must form as basis for all human rights activism.

Creation and distribution of wealth in a human society with individual rights and choice should be the basis of social development. Many of the crimes are generated when an item is not available to a member as his right or as his choice.

However, there will be difference in wealth accumulation by one to another based on inheritance, mental capacity, capacity for hard work, greed; and fetish for wealth. We should accept this variance or let me say these reasons for variance. However, deterrent should be provided by the society for acquiring additional physical wealth by snatching, looting, cheating or by illegal or immoral ways.

We may even ignore wealth accumulation by some individuals. As long as it is to provide for some kind of future emergency or future sustenance; it is meaningful, has a purpose. But over and above this need, additional accumulation of wealth is only for mental satisfaction and is notional. It does not serve the individual and does not harm the society or state if kept idle.

Let us take a practical example. Assume an individual has Rs. 10 crore as wealth. For all his current and personal needs he can spend Rs. 2 crore. Beyond this, Rs. 8 crore is useless to him except giving mental satisfaction. Can he eat more? Can he wear more? Can he have items beyond the luxury goods technologically available? Answer to all these are categorical NO. The additional wealth is probably in some form of negotiable instruments, in modern days in some sort of paper or computer records. How does it harm the society or state as long as he is not creating some sort of nuisance? Hence, we should ignore such cases. Think of all needs taken care of society of one billion people. All such idle accumulations are microscopic and useless. As a British comic writer put it 'many men of course became extremely rich, but this was perfectly natural and nothing to be ashamed of because no one was really poor, at least no one worth speaking of.'

The above discussion happened on individual's wealth which is distributed by the society or nation to its members/ citizens. Really, discussion was on distribution of wealth as a comparison of wealth of citizens. This will lead to very narrow definition of wealth and its distribution, but it is very important one. There are many ways in which distribution of this type of wealth can be analyzed. Compare the combined wealth of the richest 10% of citizens to the combined wealth of poorest 10%. Wealth inequality metrics of a nation has always been an issue of paramount importance to individuals, societies and nations. Many of the political systems evolved at different times based on debates and ideologies–Mercantilism, Capitalism, Communism, Socialism, all these 'isms' have the core issue of distribution of wealth. Even in India scripture as old as Mahabharata, analyses merits and demerits of *Sangh Rajya* (centralized, akin to Communism) and *Gana Rajya* (decentralized, akin to Democracy).

There are national assets which do not belong to any particular citizen. Roads, railways, factories, rivers, forests, educational and research institutions etc. do not belong to any one citizen but are definitely part of National Wealth. These assets also need to be considered during distribution of wealth to various regions of a nation, especially if the nation is very vast. For a small nation like Singapore or Hong Kong the regional distribution of wealth may not be an issue, but in a country as vast as India, it makes tremendous meaning. Regional imbalances in distribution of National Wealth i.e. common assets may become cause of local unrest or dissatisfaction of citizens with severe consequential outcomes.

The discussion on National Wealth will not be complete unless a few gray areas are touched upon.

Is looting or economic exploitation of another nation to create wealth is ethical or permissible? In olden days, the answer was yes; it was part of the governing process. In modern times, it is considered unethical and immoral; but the strong and powerful nations employ and practice this process of wealth creation all the time. Outwardly the professed projection is at great variance to the actual actions. Sometimes some nations do it brazenly even today. This will continue to happen and hence instead of wasting time and resources in fighting for correction, it will be prudent to enhance and bolster the defence muscles. That is the only way, and it is an old one, to bring safety and prosperity to the citizens.

Why agricultural produce is part of national wealth? The produce gets consumed by the citizens in a short period. It is national wealth since it fulfills citizens' primary need of food.

By the same token as food, are prostitutes national wealth? Yes, as human capital, they are wealth, though not utilized properly if the male to female ratio for the nation is not adverse. However, just for example, if there are only 30 adult females for every 100 adult males, then the female prostitutes will become necessary in the society for satisfying a primary need and will become part of the national wealth. Reverse will also be true; just for example, that is if there are only 20 adult males for every 100 adult females, then male prostitutes will become national wealth. During Mauryan period in India, Kautilya in his book *Arthasashtra* enumerates in detail, duties and responsibilities of the 'Superintendent of Prostitutes' in the government. It is clear from his writing that, at that time the prostitutes were not only for king and courtesans but for the pleasure of the citizens too and part of the governmental administration.

Deposits made in foreign banks by the citizens, will be part of the national wealth since the deposits in foreign banks can be made only in foreign currency, like dollars or euro etc. and can be used for purchasing goods or services as resource for the citizens. But if it is in secret accounts then it is idle wealth for the nation to which the citizen belongs, but is wealth of the nation in which the bank is situated/belongs. How and when it is loss for the nation to which the citizen belongs, will be taken up in the chapter on exports and imports.

At the end of this chapter on wealth, it may be appropriate to say that the politicians, economists, policy makers, policy implementers must start thinking in terms of wealth creation instead of poverty eradication in a short period.

Summary

- *Generation of National Wealth is of primary importance for removal of poverty. This makes India richer too.*
- *Judicious and equitable distribution of national wealth to the citizens is necessary for removal of poverty.*
- *A regional imbalance in distribution of national wealth is fraught with severe political and national consequences.*

There are only 4 methods of generation of national wealth:

(a) Extraction/use of what is found/grown on earth surface.

(b) Mining below or above earth's surface.

(c) Production

(d) Loot/Exploitation

Chapter - 7

POPULATION

China is not only formidable; it is also building its own economic infrastructure. Just a few years from now, China will rival the U.S. and the European Union in global market power. It already has surpassed us in population.

—Jo Ann Emerson

Member of the 'U.S. House of Representatives'

Future belongs to those nations, having large populations since their wealth will be the greatest and the military might will be formidable; if there are awareness and urgency of using the human capital. The days of guns is fading from the horizon and now the economic development will be at centre stage of competitions between nations.

People lament, our population is so high, our population growth is so high, what any government can do, poverty increases faster than whatever extra is done, produced and created.

To these persons, the earnest request will be to start thinking; kindly do not repeat what others are saying. Don't look from western eyes. What are they preaching to you is not truth, they know it but are so scared of you that they dare not utter the truth.

If higher population is a curse, then why are the followings happening.

- The US admit some over 700000 individuals every year as permanent residents.
- Australia admitted very substantial numbers of foreign nationals in 1980s.
- Canada if one is willing is much easier to shift to.
- Japan gives a Toyota car as present for a couple having children more than four.

Why these countries take additional people? To work, more people bigger the economy. Why European Union was formed? It was to compete with China, India and USA.

Humans are essential resource of a nation

And so India has the second largest human resource. This is a boon and not a curse. And this is so because India is close to equator. A glance at the world population density map on earth makes it clear that the density is maximum in a band along with equator. Away from equator beyond this band, population density decreases. This natural phenomenon is due to abundance of food availability and less severe climatic conditions.

India's old epic *Mahabharata* brings out this concept most aptly.

> "The one that is beautiful to eyes, where the soil has strength to produce more grains, has unique and exotic minerals and where all living beings reside; that land is told to be the best."
>
> –Mahabharat, *AshtaPanchasatmoadhya, Sutra 2.*

'Theory of Population' by English scholar Dr. Thomas Robert Malthus (1776–1834) that population when unchecked increases in geometrical ratio whereas subsistence increases only in arithmetical ratio, was eventually dismissed for its failure to take into account technological advances in agriculture and food production. Rather, nations seem to follow statement of controversial American ecologist Garret Hardin (1915-2003) "of course a positive growth rate might be taken as evidence that a population is below its optimum'. The predicted/ projected population growth rate of some of the other big and considered developed nations for 2009-2050 is comparable to India as the table shows.

Table 3: Population Growth

Country	Population year 2009 (million)	Population year 2050 (million)	Growth Rate
India	1171	1748	49 %
USA	307	439	43 %
Australia	22	34	55 %

Here, it may be appropriate to quote the Anglo-Irish writer Oliver Goldsmith (1730–1774):

"I was ever of the opinion, that the honest man who married and brought up a large family, did more service than he who continued single, and only talked of population."

India should be proud that it is a nation of over one billion people. India should have celebrated crossing the one billion mark. One billion people in one human society, in one nation, putting efforts to the society's upliftment, other small nations have to be envious of the potential wealth generation.

If India harnesses 1.2 billion individuals constructively, think of the production level in each spheres and the amount of creation of wealth.

Let us go to the numbers game.

	Nation A (UK)	Nation B (India)
Population	61 million	1200 million
Work Force*	31 million	525 million
Labour Hours**	(74.4 billion)	1260 billion)

*Work force is 'Adults in working age'.

**No. of labour hours is based on 8 hours/day/person; 300 days/year.

The difference between the two nations' labour hours availability is 1185 billion or 1.85 trillion labour hours. This difference is huge. If we assume every thing else is equal, the production capacity of nation B is 17 times of that nation A and the difference being 1185 billions. Let us visualize the difference between the two nations.

	Nation A (UK)	Nation B (India)
If it takes one hour to assemble a TV, if all workforce is assembling TV, then annual production.	74.4 billion	1260 billion

It shows the proportion of wealth generation. Nation B has gigantic potential of wealth generation compared to nation A.

	Nation A (UK)	Nation B (India)
If each person wears one underwear and needs four per year, annual market for underwear..	244 million	4800 million

Nation B has 20 times bigger domestic market for undergarments compared to nation A. This example shows the size of the domestic market.

	Nation A (UK)	Nation B (India)
At a production rate of 100 meters of cloth per hour per person with aid of machine, yearly production of cloth. (meter)	7.44 trillion	126 trillion

The example points that capacity of nation B to produce primary goods of daily use is tremendous compared to nation A.

The above comparisons make it amply clear that Nation A's production capacity and market both are mini's compared to nation B, especially when we look at the difference figures. In first case a difference of 1185 billions, in second example a difference of 4.5 billions, in the third case a difference of 118,000 billions (118 trillions). By this comparison actually America, Germany, Britain, France, Australia are miniscule production centers and also very small markets compared to India. Though this is true only if all the potential manpower resource is fully harnessed.

India has so much of human resource that it will be easily able to feed, clothe, shelter and provide all luxury goods to all the members of the nation and even much more in excess if its citizens wish to.

It means India should be rich, not poor, its citizens should be well fed and not a single member hungry for food, it should have clothing and shelter for everybody and it is just a question of a simple decision that yes, as a nation, it will have all this for every citizen of India. It does not need money, and whatever is needed, India has plenty of those. Money is not wealth or resource. India has enough of resources and India has to just create wealth by using the resources which it has. It just requires simple decision and willpower to implement, by the government/governments. Let the decision be made at this juncture. Methodology of implementation will be discussed later in the book.

For poverty removal, wealth creation is necessary. And it is important for every nation to remember the basic dictum of *Atharvaveda*:

"The nation can grow and prosper only if the population is healthy and strong, both physically and morally."

Summary

- *The domestic market and production potentials are directly proportional to the quantum of the population.*
- *Larger the population, higher the potential for wealth generation.*
- *Nations with sizeable populations will be wealthier and mighty in future.*

There is no need to worry or lament on the size or growth of population of a nation. Proper utilization of the population as a resource for generating wealth to the citizens will remove poverty of the citizens.

Chapter - 8

Exports and Imports

The great nations have always acted like gangsters, and the small nations like prostitutes.

—Stanley Kubrick in *The Guardian.*

Currency exchange rate and aid are the two best, most effective and civilized way of exploitation of poor nations conspired by developed nations.

Exports and Imports are necessary evils and boons of the modern day globalization.

Imports are necessary to keep citizens satisfied psychologically in these days of too much of communication and exposures available to citizens to choose from.

Also from technology developments and quality improvements and sometimes to take advantage of volume manufacturing, imports are necessary.

Imports are also necessary to fill the gap of requirements but no availability inside the country, example nuclear fuel or certain technologies or certain metals not mined inside the country.

Some food items and medicines also may need imports. And to maintain imports, a country needs foreign exchange and/or goods barter system. Barter system is always not feasible and to overcome the shortcomings of the barter system;

foreign exchange system was evolved. And to earn foreign exchange a country needs to export. Export is the only major long range method of earning foreign exchange. Other methods could be tourism, aid, donation, loans or repatriation by the ethnic population abroad.

Loss of Wealth by Export to Developed Nations

But any export to the countries having stronger currency is always disadvantageous. [By the way it is a subtle method of looting by having stronger currency.] Let us take example of exporting to the USA. The USA has a currency which is much stronger to Rupee. One dollar today (April, 2009) is Rs 50 as per official exchange rate.

However, as per purchasing power parity (PPP), one dollar is equivalent to Rs. 10.

Now let us assume,

- Cost of production of an item getting exported = Rs. 100
- Based on PPP, the same item should be exported to USA for at least = Rs 100/10 = US $ 10
- But based on official exchange rate, the item will get exported to USA for = Rs. 100/50 = US$ 2

The profit margin has been excluded from the above calculation just to show the concept. Though the item should have fetched at least US$ 10, but actually it is fetching only US$ 2. What happens to the difference of US$ 8? The country, which manufactured and exported, put in the efforts and resources equivalent to US$ 10, but got only US$ 2 and lost US$ 8. On Rs. 100/- worth export made, the exporting country lost Rs. 80/-.

But the importing country in this case has underpaid by US$ 8 and USA citizens enjoy this additional but free US$ 8 worth goods and services. On paying US$ 2, they are getting

US$ 10 i.e. 5 times more. At national level, it is huge loss to the citizens of the exporting country like India. It is equivalent to exploitation or looting the country which is exporting by the developed country. One may even say that the vulgar and wasteful life style of American citizens is being maintained by the hard work of citizens of Japan, China, Taiwan, India and many other countries. But definitely not by hard work of the citizens of European countries since Euro is stronger than US$ but not much. The analysis may show that the white world countries have near currency parity, only God knows why?

Coming back to the discussion, it gets proven that it is foolish to export to USA, Europe, Canada or Australia, which have made their currencies stronger (whatever may be the means of making it stronger) to the currencies of the developing world. Not only is that, by exporting to these countries, the weaker currency country is helping in making the other country's currency stronger and stronger. The citizens of the countries with stronger currencies have more time to work on more sophisticated items and developments since supplies from developing world at throw away prices take care of more mundane daily necessities.

A back of envelope calculation will show the mammoth transfer of wealth from India to the developed world due to exports and imports.

January, 2010 export=$ 14,343 million

January, 2010 import=$ 24,705 million

- Total dollar to be earned by India to keep the trade going for January, 2010= $ 24,705 million
- As shown earlier, for every $ 2 earning, India looses approximately Rs. 80 worth of national wealth.
- For Jan, 2010, India's National Wealth Loss
  = Rs. 24,705 x 40 million = Rs. 98820 crore

- At this rate, Annual Loss of National Wealth due to export/import in dollar terms

  = Rs. 98820 x 12

  = Rs. 1185840 crore

(a) India must avoid unnecessary consumption of imported items. For the month of January 2010 the fuel oil imports grew by 56%. Will India sustain such growth of imports? Besides use of fuel oil for industrial use, a major portion is used for personal transport. Can it be cut down? Real truth is that poor are working harder so that some percentage of population can enjoy the luxury of personal transport. It does not mean that cars should not be there. It does mean that let car and fuel oil availability be purely under free market democratic set-up and mechanism and no subsidy of any sort is provided on this. The fuel oil and car has been taken as an example. Similar cases will be in abundance in all areas.

(b) A country of India size must fight unjust international obligations and must not succumb to pressure, or just ignore such obligations, when it comes to meeting the basic needs of its citizens.

Take for example sugar export and import. For the year 2007-08 and 2008-09 the sugar exports were 46.84 lakh metric tons and 33.34 lakh metric tons. This was when the citizens in India had to pay exorbitant price in the domestic market for their own consumption.

Similarly, for 2008-09 the foodgrains export was 65 lakh metric tons, vegetables export worth Rs. 4.39 lakh crore, processed foods worth Rs. 3.89 lakh crore, even pulses export was 1.36 lakh tons. Under what international obligations were these exports made? For farmers benefit or for some businessmen to make money with the government help on exports by additional benefits on agricultural exports. One has to remember that these food items and many more such food items were exported when India was witnessing double digit food inflation.

How Developed Nations' Currencies are Stronger

The manufactured parts supplies from developing world make their finished goods (assembled) cheaper and that is what makes their currencies stronger.

Best quality food supplies from the developing world at throwaway prices makes their labour costs cheaper in their own currencies and so, their currencies become the stronger currency.

Most of these stronger currency countries have very little arable or irrigated agricultural lands and are having extreme cold climates not suitable for agriculture. How come, the food items are so cheap in their own currencies? Example:

In USA:

- Basmati Rice (exported from India or Pakistan) is approximately $ 10 for 5 kg.
- Pulses are $1 to $4 for 1 kg.
- Cooking oils $ 1.50 to $3.50 per litre.
- Milk approximately $ 2 for 4 litre.
- Wheat flour approximately $2 for 1kg.
- Water melon big size $4 to $8 for one.
- During season, good quality apples are sold at $ 8 for 10 - 15 kg.
- In a good restaurant $ 8 to $ 20 per person for a good filling meal.
- Grocery bill for a person for a month varies from $150 to $500 depending on place.

It is to be noted that median income per person per month for USA is more than $2000.

Also, stronger currencies countries will come and give advice to the developing nations on fiscal disciplines, advantages of no deficit budgets, how to increase exports, aid for various things etc., etc. But if you look at their own budgets, all those things will have no sanctity. America's budget deficits during various years are given below.

Table 4: USA National Debt indicating Budget Deficit

For USA:

Year	Addition to National Debt $ billion	National Debt $ billion	% of GDP
2005	523	7905	64.6
2006	536	8451	65.0
2007	459	8950	65.6
2008	1017	9985	70.2
2009 (est.)	1750	12867	90.4
2010 (est.)	1800	14456	**98.1**
2011 (est.)		15674	**101.0**

Why America never bothered to have fiscal discipline is because imports are giving the luxurious life to its citizens.

Devalued Currency and Dependence on Export makes a Developing Nation Vulnerable

Further, the exporting countries of the developing world become more prone to crisis situations at the whim of the countries with stronger currencies. Rather, more the developing nation exports to a developed nation and more the developing nation devalues its currency compared to the currency of the developed nation to have more exports to the developed nation; more the developing nation becomes vulnerable to manipulations by the developed nation–politically, economically, and psychologically. Without going into too many of detailed examples, we will take one simple example but very effective to show the point.

Food items are part of the exchange rate finalization. Labour is considered cheap after applying the official exchange rate in the developing nation. Food seems very cheap in the developing nation after official conversion rate is applied.

(a) Country X is a developing nation with very weak currency.

(b) Country Y is a developed country with very strong currency compared to X.

(c) Currency of X is Xc and Currency of Y is Yc.

(d) Let us assume Yc = 50 Xc officially

(e) Let us consider that in country X, one has to pay on an average 1000 Xc for food items consumption during a month. When it is converted to Yc, it works out to 20 Yc. In country Y, on average one has to pay 200 Yc for a month's food item. Though it will be a fallacy to assume that the food is cheaper in the country X, for export price calculation it is working out that in country X the food is cheaper by 10 times. That makes the labour cheaper in the eyes of the importing country Y.

(f) After sometime, importing country Y is not happy with country X for some reason. In country X, country Y strategically gets articles published in magazines and in newspapers, that there is going to be food shortages all over the world for many years to come, there is not enough food for all the population in the world, food is very cheap in country X, gives data as explained above. What will be the result? The prices of food items will go up in country X. Once, the food prices jump up in country X, the labour cost goes up besides political and social turmoil. The industry in country X suffers, and price rise happens all across. The exports become uncompetitive compared to some other country. But who is the biggest sufferer? The citizens of country X. Nobody cares.

(g) This strategy is adopted by many multinationals too.

The disadvantage of weaker currency works for travel too. The country X citizens will not be able to travel to country Y because they will need 50 times more money due to official exchange rate. Whereas, the country Y citizens will enjoy travelling to country X, since there currency will give 50 times more the currency of country X and for them the travel to country X will become dirt cheap.

So by managing to keep stronger currency by some of the countries, it is most subtle way of using labour and natural resources of the developing world to their advantage.

The country which goes on exporting more and more to the countries having stronger currencies is doing injustice to its own citizens of depriving of the fruits of labour and natural resources.

The example quoted by some, of prosperity of Japan, South Korea, and now even China is full of pitfalls. The quality of life of citizens in these countries is not the same as that of the developed world. The common citizens in these countries do not enjoy the same size of accommodation, quality of food or freedom of resources to enjoy life.

Hence, exports must be kept to minimum and just only to meet or to pay for the imports. Imports must be kept to minimum so as necessity to export is less and less.

And if a country wishes that its citizens enjoy the best possible quality of life, it must keep its imports to the bare minimum, importing only most essential requirements. This is less painful for the big countries having rich natural resources like India, China, Indonesia or South Africa.

It may be better idea to export and import to and from countries having parity in currency/official exchange rate. Currency Xc = Ac = Bc = Dc.

In this case county X could export and import to countries A, B, C and D and even grow the trade. If not this, trade to be developed with the countries having official exchange rate very close to the PPP exchange rate.

Today what is being followed by the developing nations is really making these countries poorer and the developed world richer. The citizens of the developed nations are enjoying better quality of life not because of their own hard work or abundance of natural resources, but, a major contribution to the same is from the developing nations.

Exports of natural resources like iron ores, mica or for that matter any mined item is making the country poorer (loss of existing wealth) and future generations will suffer. Exports of agricultural item are criminal as long as there is one citizen hungry even for a day for the reasons of nonavailability of food or if he/she cannot afford food. It is unethical if a child is undernourished.

Imports from Developed World are equally exploitive and subsidizes living in the developed world

General impression is that weaker currency discourages imports and so helps to maintain trade deficit. This impression and philosophy is erroneous. If it really helped then America would have devalued dollar every year since there trade deficit runs in trillions. If it helped, Euro and Pounds would have been devalued many times. These countries never devalue their currencies. Because opposite is true for them. Since these currencies are officially very strong (result of a system of determination of exchange rate created by these countries); imports from rest of the world having many times weaker currencies, adds wealth to these strong currencies' nations. These nations' (having strong currencies) citizens get the goods and services without working for the same. Their citizens enjoy life and the developing countries' citizens put in the hard work and do not get even the daily necessities of life.

But for developing nations having very weak currencies like India (1 US Dollar = Rs. 50) imports do the exactly reverse i.e. make the exporting nation having stronger currency wealthier. How does it happen?

Simply, by the exchange rate:

Let us assume that India imports 100 Euros worth item, we will ignore the profit content to keep the calculation simpler. At present exchange conversion rate of one Euro is nearly Rs. 80.00.

Indian importer pays 100 Euro (Rs. 8000 at official exchange rate.) for the item. Actual conversion rate based on purchasing power will be much lower let us say one Euro equals Rs. 5.00. So, for 100 Euro the Indian importer should have paid Rs. 500/-. But he pays Rs. 8000 to get 100 Euros. Hence, the difference of Rs. 7500 worth Indian wealth gets paid to the country exporting. This wealth transfer has not happened at the time of the import. This wealth transfer has happened while exporting to get 100 Euro. For Rs. 500 worth item India paid Rs. 8000/-. India paid 8 times more. The European exporting country earned a profit margin of 1500% on the sale price over and above the normal profit. It is besides the fact that in the name of technology their prices of goods are already huge.

These countries with officially stronger currencies will try to persuade, argue, bribe, threat and use force to open the domestic markets of the developing nations having weaker currencies. Because that is how these countries are wealthy. The day the exchange rate is forced to be one to one or their currency being made weaker, the same nations will loose interest in exporting or opening up of the market.

Summary

- *Any trade with those nations whose currency exchange rates are very adverse, like US Dollars, Canadian Dollars, Australian Dollars, Euro; is detrimental to the nation whose currency is weaker. Hence trade with such countries is to be limited to absolute necessities only.*
- *Export by a nation whose currency is weaker, is providing subsidy to the citizens of that nation whose currency is stronger. The amount of subsidy is proportional to the difference in the official currency exchange rate.*
- *Import from the countries whose currencies are stronger, is overpaying than the real value of the commodity/goods or services. The quantum of overpayment is proportional to the difference in the official exchange rate of the two currencies.*
- *Guru mantra will be to develop, encourage, solicit, slightly subsidize trade with the countries whose official currency exchange rate is one or nearer to one.*
- *In this global age, the biggest fiscal endeavour of the government is to be or to do all that is required to bring official exchange rates to one. Even purchasing power parity currency conversion is full of flaws and anyway is not followed.*

A big and resourceful country like India has to accelerate internal wealth creation using internal resources.

Keep the windows open for fresh air; but do not open the door for others to walk in with cunning persuasions and sweet talks or do not open the windows without putting safety grills so as the others do not get into your house stealthily.

Chapter - 9

REMOVAL OF POVERTY

In a country well governed, poverty is something to be ashamed of. In a country badly governed, wealth is something to be ashamed of.

—Confucius

Creation of wealth on national level at super fast speed is the key to remove poverty in totality and make a Richer India.

The priorities will be:

(a) Meeting the *basic requirement* of food, shelter and clothing for each and every individual of the nation.

(b) Education to sustain the above process of removal of the poverty.

(c) Creation of other types of wealth at national level using all the available resources especially the human population.

Real removal of poverty will mean

Every citizen will have

- Good quality and nourishing food.
- Decent Clothing
- Reasonable Shelter
- Graduate Education
- Household Accessories: electricity, utensils, cooking gas, telephone, washing machine, dishwasher, TV, computer,

broadband connectivity, mobile, furniture, bed and bed sheets, pillow and pillow covers etc.

- Quality surroundings: fresh air, playgrounds, parks, community halls, libraries etc.
- Neat and Clean Travel: by road, rail or air.

Making food available to every citizen

Grains: Grains are the main energy source and needs to be provided to, made available to each and every citizen. To do this, enough grain production, widespread quick distribution systems are the two key essential processes.

Which are the grains considered as essential staple food?

—Wheat, Rice, Pulses?

In India, most, nay all of the citizens do eat vegetarian meals and dairy products. Some may add or supplement their meals with eggs and meat or fish. This is since India is a hot country in the tropical zone. Foodgrains are daily essential and substantial inputs for the citizens' diet. Other grains besides wheat, rice and pulses are used but in very small quantities and the production of these grains is also on decline since demand is dwindling.

Table 5: Foodgrains Availability

	Consumption Kg./Year/ Person	India's Requirement (Billion Kg.)	India's Production (Billion Kg.)	India's Shortage (Billion Kg.)
Wheat	60	72	76	No Shortage
Rice	60	72	94	No Shortage
Pulses	60	72	15	57

The agriculturists may dispute the average consumption figures as shown above. It works out to just 493 gm. of grains per day. There are at least 3 meals a day when grains are used presently. A healthy young male doing physical work will consume more than that. However considering women and children, average is kept lower.

Although, there is doubt on estimates of the actual production figures. If wheat and rice is produced in excess of national requirements, why the prices of these grains keep rising every year and that too in a disproportionate fashion when compared to inflation figures ?

Also what are we going to do for wheat and rice production as population is rising every year but the production of wheat and rice have reached plateau. There is hardly any substantial increase in production over the last few years.

As far as pulses are concerned the scenario is pathetic. There is huge shortage of pulses required for consumption in India and the actual availability as per production figure in India is very less.

India needs more quantity of pulses to be consumed because Indians prefer to be vegetarians for most of the days of a year. And, at present, pulses are the major protein supplies to Indian citizens. It also needs to be emphasized that pulses are the major protein supplies to the Indian children; who are growing and growth of physique and brain both require necessary proteins.

And how are we meeting the requirement at national level? By increased price of the pulses per kg. so that households cannot afford to buy pulses and the demand meets the supply by this mechanism. And we never bother what will be the future of this country when children do not get enough of protein.

In our democracy the retail purchasing price rates for pulses are increasing in leaps and bounds. At the current prices, pinch is felt even by the middle class families in India when it comes to dal (pulses) purchases/ or for items in that category like rajma, chana etc.

Production of pulses at national level has been decreasing instead of going up. *Pulses supply today is the biggest national crisis in the Indian history.*

And import is not the solution, since pulses are not produced widely in other nations except Pakistan. In case of import of foodgrains or for that matter any food item is only giving double the profit to some individuals; unless exports of foodgrains and food items is totally banned for long term (20 years or so). In the current scenario, export subsidy (sometimes over 100%) is earned on the exports, because of exports domestic shortages happen and prices go up, then government imports the same at higher prices. What a bad governance of food security management?

There are five possible solutions on the shortage of pulses supply vis-a-vis requirement;

1. Increase in the irrigated land availability and that additional land goes for cultivation of pulses.

2. Encouragement to eat meat and poultry in the cold areas of Himalayas and increase in availability of these items.

3. Encouragement to eat fish in the coastal areas and making available the same.

4. Creation of artificial lakes all over the country. This will help increase the irrigated land area, and also add to increase the production of fish and to some extent help in production of more meat and poultry.

5. Focus on availability of food supplements in the form of fruits and nuts. Though these items are not really substitutes to foodgrains.

Anyone only of the above will not give the solution to the problem. A well planned actions oriented formulation of strategy consisting all the above will only bring out the solution over a period of time. However, central government and state governments must realize that it is a critical issue which needs emergency approach to solve.

The above discussion brings out one more issue.

Grains production in India has probably reached a plateau. Population is still increasing and should not be discouraged, since it is resource and power. Unless technological breakthrough happens i.e. reduction in cycle time for the crop to grow, flower and seed, the scenario is very serious and critical. This type of technological breakthrough is by genetic modifications and should never be implemented without rigorous, long term controlled tests and evaluations of 30 to 40 years. If any decision is taken on such discoveries in haste, there is huge risk of making the whole nation's human population crippled, or physically weak, or mentally weak or impotent or sterile (i.e. incapable of producing children), or stressful etc. etc. Any abnormality including human genetic modification can happen accidentally affecting the whole population.

So what are the other methods of covering of the gap? As touched upon earlier, food supplements are the items to cover the gaps in availability, as well as necessary to wholesome nourishments.

Following are the major food supplements not being in the grain category.

- Milk and dairy items
- Meat
- Eggs
- Fish
- Vegetables
- Fruits and Nuts

India produces annually 1000 lakh tons of milk (highest in the world), 1500 lakh tons of fruits and vegetables (second largest), 2040 lakh tons foodgrains (third largest), 63 lakh tons of fish (third largest), 4890 lakh poultry and 4520 crore eggs. But irony is that with all this over 50% of Indians are partially hungry or undernourished.

Milk and Dairy items: Production in India is equivalent to 100 billion Kg. of milk per year. This works out to 86 kg. of milk per year per citizen or 235 grams per day per citizen. In developed countries the availability works out to 1500 grams to 2500 grams per day per person. In India we need not reach to this high level of availability and consumption but 235 grams also is too low when availability of protein in the form of pulses is pathetically low. Even if we put 1000 grams of milk equivalent availability of dairy products per citizen per day; we need production of 438 billion kg. every year and annual growth rate in production to match the population growth rate.

At present level of production there is shortage of milk and dairy production equivalent to 338 billion kg. per year i. e. actually we need to increase the production 4 to 5 times of current annual production.

So, there is dire necessity and there is good scope to increase production of milk and milk products. Space to keep the milk producing animals (cows, buffalos) is not a problem but the feedstock to raise and maintain the livestock is to be made available. Focus has to be kept on production of grass and fodder for the animals to eat.

At present roughly Rs. 1000 crore worth of feedstock is being exported. First thing government can do is stop the export of grass, fodder and feedstock completely. There is no sense in earning foreign exchange by exporting feedstock when the citizens are not getting proper food and nourishment.

However, grass and feedstock should not be produced sacrificing grains production.

Creating lakes and canals to increase irrigated land on those land areas which cannot be used for agriculture, will produce grassland for the cows and buffalos to graze.

There are acres and acres of example innumerable barren hills in south and in Vindhyas in north (like hillocks at Ahmednagar in Maharashtra). By explosive blasting at the foothills and then removing the loosened earth by excavating machines (now powerful ones are being made in India) and spreading of thick plastic cloth, a lake can be created just in a few days. Rain water can be harvested and used for agriculture, creating grassland, producing fish and planting trees in the nearby areas.

Just imagine three or four lakes around a barren desolatory hillock will change the skyline of that area. Putting grass carpets once around and over the hill and watering the same on regular basis using the pumps fitted at the artificial lakes will make the whole area green throughout the year. The same could be used for raising more number of cows and buffaloes in and around the hill. This way dramatic increase in production of milk and milk products can be done without touching any existing grain producing land. Fish culture could be developed in the lake. If there is fertile land nearby starving for water will add to produce more grains too.

For the rainwater falling on the hills to collect into the lakes, the artificial lakes are to be created at the foothills. Big size plastic cloth to be developed by plastic items manufacturers and joining methods too. This cloth spreading is of utmost importance in this process to retain the rain water for the whole year.

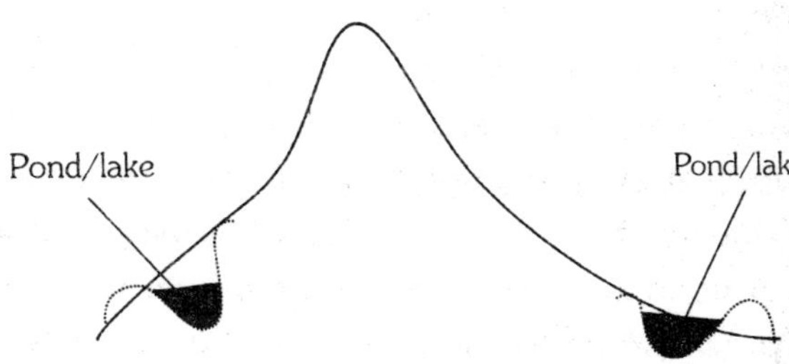

The size and depth of the lakes will also be an important factor so that water evaporation throughout the year does not make it dry. Water must remain in the lake for the whole year so that fish culture is progressed from year to year. Creation of this sort of ponds/lakes is to be done in such a fashion that water loss due to evaporation is less. For this open surface area of the pond/lake has to be less to reduce water loss due to evaporation. Depth of the pond/lake is to be more so that water remains available for the whole year.

Just as a guide, minimum depth of ten meters (or some standardized depth) may be made compulsory. This will determine the drilling depth for the explosives and the amount of explosives etc. Catchment area for the pond/lake also needs to be determined so that enough water flows in to fill the same for the whole year. If necessary, some sort of banking on the hill may be created to ensure the flow of water into the lake.

Over and above, in conjunction of the lakes and canals, widespread use of drip irrigation technology in water shortage areas will preserve water as well as give food production.

We should not get complacent that India is the largest producer of milk in the world. The availability figure for every citizen of the country is dismal when compared to other countries. We must strive and do everything possible to increase many fold the production of dairy items. It is a necessity for the food security and future of the nation based on the quality of its citizen.

Meat: Especially red meat is not good for health and much so in warm countries like India. It does not mean that India should stop production of meat and chicken and other meat products. In a country which has largest number of hungry or malnutritioned citizens, food is precious and must be consumed. Meat in moderate quantity will not do great harm and especially in the hilly region of Himalayas; having cold climate throughout the year. Rather in these areas we encourage the people to consume more of this as part of diet so that pressure on pulses availability is reduced in the other areas. Meat and chicken have high degree of proteins.

But great care must be taken at national level that meat consumption in other areas does not grow. Meat producing cattle consume great amount of grains. Over and above, cattle release methane which is more potent in global warming than carbon dioxide. Considering meat's less efficient production process, harmful affect on climate and health hazards; it will be wiser to discourage this food item except in very extreme cold climate regions. Also preservation of meat in warm climate, which most of the regions in India have, requires refrigeration to lower temperatures and hence energy consumption is higher for preservation. This tends to make this food more resource consuming and expensive.

Production, Processing and Preservation techniques (3 Ps of Meat) for meat and chicken products to be encouraged; scientific preservation techniques to be introduced on a larger scale in the hilly regions of our country i.e. Kashmir, Laddakh, Himachal Pradesh, Uttarakhand, Sikkim and some of the North-east States.

Eggs: As food supplement eggs provide good amount of protein required for growth and for sustenance. Eggs substitute to some extent the protein requirement from pulses. Since pulses are in great shortage, eggs consumption offsets that though impact of the eggs on overall national protein supply and meeting requirement on the national level is miniscule. Its impact is very small on daily basis. But any food supplement is important to bridge the gap.

Egg production and consumption suffered a great deal after the Bird Flue disease. It is doubtful that the situation will improve, since occasional sporadic occurrence of the disease is still continuing. However, total poultry production and consumption is on a growth path. This has to be substantially increased.

Exports of poultry products including eggs to other countries is to be stopped immediately. Irony of the scenario is that the main feedstock in poultry raising is soyabean cake and India exports over 24 million tonnes of soyabean cake to Europe. In India the prices of chicken and eggs only go on rising. Government authorities get comfort that the eggs prices in India is lower than America and Europe but they forget that this calculation is based on unrealistic foreign exchange rates and average Indian having median income cannot afford to eat eggs and chicken at the current prices. As usual at present, the government policies on food, subsidized food for the citizens of other nations and there is no care for the hunger of the citizens of this nation.

Fish: Production, Processing and Preservation techniques (3P's of Fish) differ from that of meat. Also not only eating fish is considered to be healthy; Indian states having sea shores have developed taste for fish. We have 7200 km. of sea coast line and fish is supplementing the protein requirement to some extent on the national level. Research must be initiated how to increase the cultivation and production of fish in the deep sea water near to the coast.

Further, by creating artificial ponds and lakes inland, fish production can be given a big boost. The idea of mass-making of ponds and lakes all over India on the barren land, presented in this book for milk production, will provide readymade source for fish production. There is great potential for increasing fish production by creating ponds and lakes. This must be pursued with full vigour. And this increase will not take away any land under grains production. Grains production is sacrosanct and the production area must never be touched leading to any reduction in grains production area.

Milk, meat, chicken, egg and fish as food will need emphasis on preservation techniques and also development of refrigerated transport and storage both in the depots and in the houses.

Fridge will be a necessity in all the homes consuming meat, chicken, fish, milk and dairy products to avoid wastage.

Vegetables: Vegetables are essential food supplements and must be consumed on daily basis for providing vitamins and minerals. The availability of vegetables to every citizen must be insured by increasing production, preservation and proper distribution.

But increasing production of vegetables is not to be done by putting more land taking away the grains production land. Grains producing land is sacrosanct and never to be touched for any other endeavour. However, in some areas of north India there are 3 crops raised in a year, one crop could be of vegetables on the grains producing land.

To increase production of vegetables, all urban parks, housing societies' gardens are to be converted to vegetable farming instead of lawns and grass. Vegetable fields also are green and soothing to eyes.

Water used for lawn will be better used for vegetables. What about evening sit-outs of residents. Sit-out on Benches in the vegetable garden will be much more pleasant and also provide stimulus to children in learning about food and nature.

However, biggest hindrance will be the logic that (a) who will do the farming and (b) it will be very difficult to farm in the public places because people will steal the vegetables and it will be difficult to manage.

For "who will do the farming?", every park and garden is to be contracted out by the municipalities and housing societies to farming contractors for production of vegetables. With all apprehensions, if this is forced, and it must be forced when there are so many hungry citizens; this will work. People will see the reason for vegetables prices within reach of everybody.

For 'people will steal the vegetables'; first of all some person, or some child will eat the stolen vegetable and when we are talking about on the national level; who eats is immaterial, as long as some citizen eats the same. Second, most parks and gardens nowadays have watchmen and thefts will not be that rampant. Make big size parks and gardens in areas newly being developed as residential areas so that the farming contractors themselves protect the same for the economic benefit. Third, as a nation we will have to create more numbers and bigger and bigger size parks and gardens for better health and reduction in future healthcare expenditures i.e. reducing of demand on resources. Of course emphasizing that all this is necessary since grain land is sacrosanct and not to be touched for any other activities and hence bigger and more number of parks and gardens in cities/towns on barren land areas, will add to sustain production of vegetables besides its good use for the maintenance of health of the citizens by providing fresh air, place for walks and exercises.

Other methodology for increasing production of vegetables will be to utilize hills which are having earth soil on the surface. Most of the Himalayan hills/mountains have fertile soil on the surface. But this vegetable production on hills have to be developed without cutting a single tree, it is possible and achievable quickly.

First, a hill adds surface land area available to a country. Let us see how and how much.

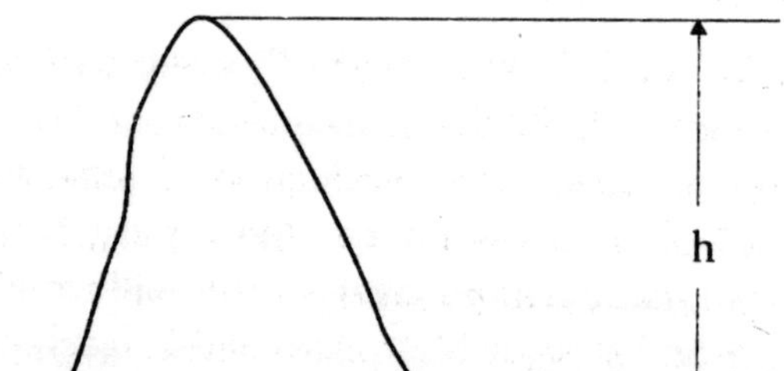

- Flat land area if the hill was not there = Fa = 0.785 d x d
- Conical Surface Land Area (excluding the flat land area if the hill was not there i.e. the base of the hill)

  = Ca = 0.785 d x sq. root of (dxd + 4 h x h)

Just assuming a mountain in the Himalayas of 1 km diameter and 1 km height as a simple cone as a simplified example:

- Flat Area= Fa = 0.785 sq. km
- Cone surface area = Ca = 1.755 sq. km
- So this hill added 1.755-0.785 = 0.97 sq. km area to the nation.

The conical surface area of the mountain will be approximately 1.755/0.785 = 2.24 times of the flat land if mountain was not there. In essence the mountain added substantially more land area to the nation. Some of the Himalayan Mountains are high and 2 km heights will not be unrealistic. If we assume 2 km. height on a 1 km diameter base:

- Flat Area = Fa = 0.785 sq. km.
- Conical surface area = Ca = 3.24 sq. km.
- 3.24/0.785 = 4.127 i.e. four times more surface area is available due to the mountain compared to if mountain was not there.

It just proves that hills, mountains add substantially to the available land of a nation.

Fortunately, India is a vast country with many hills, mountain ranges and that makes India a much bigger land country than only considering flat land. And this additional surface land of hills and mountains to be utilized for many purposes and without sacrificing the grain land area.

One use will be to substantially enhance production of vegetables but without cutting any tree.

Some mountains have tall trees like in Himalayan ranges –vegetable farming technology needs to be developed and extended to the communities living in those areas.

The hills and mountains which do not have tall trees but have somewhat fertile surface soil to be developed also for the vegetables production. This will require quick research and making water available. Again rain water harvesting to be developed and it will be worth to put resources in this direction.

Fruits: This is one food supplement which has the greatest potential to remove hunger in India. And it is known to everybody that its nourishment is essential for both body and mind.

If we concentrate on increasing the availability of fruits in India, it can be said without any doubt, that the coming and the future generations of India will be able bodied and intelligent.

- Geographical area of India = 3287590 sq. km
- Land Area = 2973190 sq. km.
- Arable Land = 1451800 sq. km.
- Irrigated Land = 558080 sq. km.
- Residential/Community/Industrial/Offices etc will occupy (assuming 200 sq.m. per person and 1.66 billion population in yr. 2050)

  = 332 billion sq.m.

  = 332000000000/(1000 x 1000) sq. km.

  = 332000 sq. km.
- Clear Area available for fruit plantation/production

  = Land Area – Arable land – Non Agri Land

  = 2973190 – 1451800 – 332000 sq. km.

  = 1189390 sq. km.

The above land area is more than combined total land area of UK, Japan and Germany (241590 + 374744 + 349223 = 965557 sq. km.).

Present non-agricultural use land is only 120 sq. m. per person. But by the year 2050, we must increase the quality of life and hence provide 200 sq.m. per citizen for housing, community centers, offices and industry. And this is what has been assumed in the above calculation.

Further, the available land difference between arable land and irrigated land i. e. 1451800 – 558 080 = 893720 sq. km. will also have fruit trees.

Further, the non agri land 332000 sq. km will also have fruit trees. And also, we have not accounted the land availability increase due to Hills and Mountains. That will add further to the land available for fruit trees.

The above proves that land availability for Fruit Tree plantation is huge and the potential to provide health food to Indian citizens is enormous. If we focus on this fruit tree plantation, Indian food security is assured for ever, irrespective of the population growth.

Let us just try to make rough estimate of, just very rough and on the conservative side, the production figure of fruits if all the available land that is not used for any other purpose, is planted with fruit trees.

First let us exclude the agri and non-agri lands and after exclusion we have 1189390 sq. km. of land. 50% of this area is hilly and mountainous and approximately two times increase in the surface area availability is considered for trees other than fruit trees to maintain ecological balance. What it means is that approximately 594700 sq. km. of land is allocated to trees other than fruit trees to maintain ecological balance in nature.

- So available land for fruit tree plantations = 1784085 sq. km.
- Assuming that a fruit tree on average will need 25 sq.m of land, possible no. of trees on the above land

= 1784085000000/25

= 71363400000 trees (71.3634 billion fruit trees)

- If each tree on an average produces 50 kg. of fruits per year;
- Annual production of fruits = 3568 billion kg.
- Availability of fruit per citizen in the year 2050=3568/1.66 = 2150 kg.
- Availability of fruit per citizen per day at the increased population level of 1.66 billion people in the year 2050 = 5.89 kg.

With the above figure will there be any hunger or shortage of food? It will be in excess multifold.

The potential of fruit trees in India

No citizen will be hungry even if we achieve one third of what is projected here. And it is feasible to achieve much more than what is projected because we have still not taken the fruit trees on the arable land and on the land for non agri purposes. Density of trees on these lands will be less but numbers will still work out huge.

Let us take a rough calculation for that too.

- Total arable land + non-agri use land = 1451800 + 332000 sq. km = 1783800000000 sq. m
- If we take only one fruit tree for 100 sq. m of land, number of fruit trees

  = 1783800000000/100 = 17838000000(17.838 billion trees)
- If we assume 50 kg. of annual fruit production per tree, annual production of fruits= 17.838 billion x 50 kg/year = 892 billion kg.
- Additional fruit availability per citizen in the year 2050 per day = 1.47 kg

- Total fruit availability per citizen per day population level of year 2050 = 5.89 + 1.47 kg.

  = 7.36 kg. of fruit/citizen per day

The above estimate is on the conservative side.

(a) Fruit trees if properly taken care give much more fruit than 50 kg. per year. A mango tree gives approx. 1000 kg. of fruits, a jack fruit gives 80-175 kg., a jamun tree 50–100 kg., date tree 80-100 kgs., tamarind 150-225 kg., aonla 100-150 kg., orange tree 100-200 fruits, mousambi 300-1000 fruits.

(b) Assumption of 25 sq. m per tree is on very much on conservative side. Except a few variety of some of the fruit trees, all others require area much less than this.

(c) Assumption of 1 tree/100 sq. m density in the arable and non agri use land is much on the lower side, if focus on planting fruit trees is kept in these areas too. Of course, without touching/affecting the land under grain production.

(d) Only thing what is not taken on the conservative side is the focus to plant fruit trees on every piece of available land.

The above projection seems to be erroneous, ludicrous! It is none of these, it is just too simplistic.

Yes, it is simplistic, all great things to be done have to be imagined in the most simplistic forms for the brain to assimilate. The above shows the direction, and impresses that if fruits production is perused vigorously, has the greatest potential to eliminate hunger from this country, eliminate malnourishment of its citizen, eliminate undernourishment of children and that too for growing population.

If fruit plantation and production is sincerely emphasized, actively pursued with imagination in India, it will feed along with existing level of grain production, will take care of many times of our present population.

Besides the above way forward, there are 'must do' rules/ policies to be followed at the national level or by central government. These are necessary to reduce hunger of citizens who are poor.

Summary

- *For removal of physical poverty, order of priority to be Food, Clothing, and Shelter.*
- *To make food available to every citizen;*

(i) *export of any type of food items to be totally banned for ever.*

(ii) *Prices of food items especially grains, vegetables and fruits to be made very low (as good as free) to the final customer i.e. every citizen.*

(iii) *Supplementary food items (meat, fish, milk, eggs, vegetables, fruits etc.) production to be increased. Exports of any input going into the production of any of the supplementary food items to be totally stopped for the next 15 years.*

- *Fruit trees plantation to be made a national campaign with sizeable resource allocation.*

Land under foodgrains cultivation to be considered sacrosanct and severe punishment to be legislated by central government for sale/allotment/use of such land for any other purpose by any individual, agency, community, panchayat, municipality or state government. Any authority resting with any agency including central and state governments for sale/allotment/use of land under foodgrains cultivation is to be withdrawn.

Chapter - 10

How to Remove Poverty in 5 Years

Never before has man had such capacity to control his own environment, to end thirst and hunger, to conquer poverty and disease, to banish illiteracy and massive human misery. We have the power to make this the best generation of mankind in the history of the world or to make it the last.

—John F Kennedy, speech (1963)

Planning and all inclusive ruthless implementation is the key to creating wealth in any nation. Equitable distribution to all citizens is government's governance. Communication and more communication is the essential ingredient to overcome conflicts during implementation of plans for creation of national wealth and equitable distribution.

What all needs to be done to remove poverty? What should be part of the detail planning? Planning process for a nation in general is to be for very long periods – 100 years, 50 years, 30 years, 20 years and for the first 5 years. These plans have to be rolling plans with every quarter reviews. Then detail planning is done for yearly targets, monthly targets and daily plans at various levels and for various departments/ agencies of governance. At present 5 year plans are made by central government but it is doubtful that a serious planning is done for even 5 years at state governments' levels. It is also doubtful that monthly and daily plans are created by any government agency.

If nation has to move forward at quick pace, it must get into culture of good planning, implementation and performance appraisal systems and processes. Even after over 60 years of independence, such wide-spread poverty speaks loudly on performance and needs to be introspected and revamping of processes are absolutely necessary.

One should never forget the axiom that once target is set, target is fulfilled. The concept of "realistic target" is erroneous and self defeating. Ambitious targets are set on visions. This is all well known and well understood in industry, then why not for a nation?

1. Food Security

Large scale mammoth planning and implementation of making food available to each and every citizen of the country.

Targets are to be per capita year wise for grains, vegetables, fruits, dairy and fisheries.

(i) Today (actual availability).

(ii) Every future year for the next 4 years.

(iii) Future 5th year, 10th year, 15th year, 20th year, 30th year, 50th year, 70th year and 100th year.

Targets have to be ambitious and by 5th year no food deficiency to remain. Food must be nutritious, healthy and well proportioned. The availability targets to be a little more (let us say 10% more) than what a dietician will recommend. The "today" column is just to show the actual availability and all of us know that none of these are available in plenty in India and so great deficiencies exist at per capita level.

Imports of food items in emergency and of specific item may be considered, but should not be the part of long term planning. India is rich in natural resources and if properly developed, it is feasible to meet the requirements of food items.

Export of food items is to be completely prohibited.

(a) **Grains availability** (production minus wastage) per individual of the population for daily consumption.

Today: 430 gram/capita

5th year: 690 gram/capita {10% growth rate}

@ Average price to citizens Rs 2/kg

It will still be much lower availability for every citizen of India than citizens of USA or China.

If one goes by the India data, the consumption of grains has been going down in India over the years. Reason is not more availability of fruits and vegetables or animal products; but it is because citizens are not able to buy due to high prices of grains. How many of us middle class can afford to buy pulses at Rs. 80-100/kg or rice at Rs. 35-50/kg? So consumption is reduced. Think of the poor or the borderline families, they have no choice but to cut on consumption. Over the years the inflation rate on food items has been too high. Citizens are just going partially hungry.

(b) **Vegetables availability** (production minus wastage) per individual of the population for daily consumption.

Today: 200 gram/capita

5th year: 400 gram/capita

@ average price to citizens Rs. 3/kg

Though national institute of Hyderabad may give lower minimum requirement (270-300 grams/day per person), latest nutritional recommendations for healthy body and excellent immunity demand more of vegetables and the country must cater to.

(c) **Fruits availability per individual** (production minus wastage) of the population for daily consumption.

Today: 100 gram/capita

5th Year: 300 gram/capita

@ average price to citizens Rs. 4/kg

Though national institute of Hyderabad may give lower minimum requirement (92 - 140 grams /day per person), latest nutritional recommendations for healthy body and excellent immunity demand more of fruits and the country must cater to.

- The above targets for vegetables and fruits and its implementation will make Indian citizen to have same level of availability as in USA or EU or even China.
- India's export of fruits and vegetables in 2007-08 was 1724573 metric tons; earning just 605 million US dollars. If the export would have not been done, it would have at least added availability of 1.5 kg of additional fruit and vegetables for every citizen during the year. When it comes to food items, we have to follow the old cliché of drops make the ocean. We have to look for every gram/capita addition of food if we have to meet the above targets.

(d) Dairy availability (production minus loss) per individual of the population for daily consumption.

Today: 250 gram/capita

5th Year: 400 gram/capita

@ average price to citizens Rs. 2/liter or Rs 2/kg

India is the largest producer of milk in the world, but substantial amount is exported even when the pricing of milk in India is such that the consumption inside the country gets restrained appreciably. That means adults do not get what they would like to have and children's physical and mental growth is sacrificed. Export of dairy (milk) and its products like butter, ghee etc. is to be prohibited.

Due to high price of milk (Rs. 25-30/liter) there is large scale adulteration happening at the expense of citizens' health. Prices are to be brought down for the reasons of affordability plus also making adulteration unattractive. Further there has to be stringent punishment for adulteration, it should be equated with cold blooded murder of many human beings. Legislation to this effect needs to be urgently passed.

> **China executes 2 for tainted milk:** China executed a dairy farmer and a milk salesman on Tuesday, the only two people sentenced to death in a scheme to water down infant formula with an industrial chemical that left at least six children dead and sickened more than three lakh people.

If China punishes by execution for milk adulteration, hang its senior official for drug adulteration; will it not be appropriate to hang the persons responsible for milk adulteration in India? Milk adulteration has become such common place in every city of India that only choice for the citizens now is left not to drink milk or consume any direct milk products. Just see the newspaper report on page 100 showing the milk adulteration situation in one city of Pune alone. And that is marginalizing the future generation of citizens. Milk is an essential intake item for children. Crime of milk adulteration is to be treated equal to sedation or war against the nation.

(e) Fisheries: India's total fish production is 6.4 million metric tons. India is the third largest producer of fish in the world and second in inland fish production. There has been good growth too over the last few years.

The potential of this sector contributing to the nation's food security is tremendous. India has over 8000 km of sea coast, over 171000 km of rivers and canals, over 2 million ha reservoirs, 2.855 million ha ponds and 14000 sq. km brackish water. By introduction of more numbers of mechanized vessels

Five Rackets Exposed This Year; NGO Demands Probe

FDA attempts to curb adulteration of milk

Swati Shinde | TNN

Pune: In the wake of the recent milk adulteration cases unearthed in the district, the Food and Drug Administration (FDA), after consulting the Pune District Co-operative Milk Producers' Federation and 150 dairy owners, prepared a 13-point precautionary draft, which has been circulated to all dairy owners in Pune, Sangli and Kolhapur districts.

Speaking to TOI on Friday, S T Patil, joint commissioner, FDA, Pune, said, "About 15 days ago, we invited all dairy owners in Pune district to discuss their problems and help find a solution to the milk adulteration issue. A 13-point draft was prepared after the discussion. This draft will be circulated to all milk producing associations, dairy owners and co-operatives."

A similar meeting was held for milk producers in Sangli and Kolhapur in early September and a similar draft was discussed and prepared for circulation to milk producers in these districts.

The draft explains the FDA rules and regulations, and the dos an don'ts when it comes to buying sealed packets of milk.

Ramesh Bhujbal, chairman of the Pune District Co-operative Milk Producers' Federation, said, "We have provided adulteration testing kits to each of these centres. We have also given very strict instructions to all milk collection centres in the district that if milk is found to be adulterated then it should not be bought."

Sadanand Godse

Arogya Sena members protest outside the collectorate recently

13-point draft to ensure purity of milk

- Milk producers must have a licence as per the Food Adulteration Act. Buyers must ensure that the seller, too, has a licence
- Manufacturing date and 'used by' date must be printed on packets
- Producers must ensure that all packets are sealed and the sides do not have any tears
- Milk producers, distributors, sellers and consumers must ensure that empty milk packets are destroyed properly
- Milk producers must keep a watch on the place where their packets are printed
- Protein test must be conducted before sealing packets
- Print the variety of milk and its price on packet. A board mentioning these details should be put outside the shop
- Provide a list of names of authorised milk agencies and the agents appointed by them to the government
- Producer must provide an identity card to his distributor and agent. The distributor in turn must provide an identity card to retail sellers and the sales boy
- Producer must appoint an inspection squad and conduct surprise visits
- The FDA must be informed immediately if milk from any collection centre is rejected
- Every collection centre must check the number of cows and buffaloes with the primary milk seller, how many yield milk and how much milk is generated daily, thus helping monitor sudden rise or decline in the supply of milk
- Centres should collect milk only after it is tested

Arogya Sena demands CBI inquiry

TIMES NEWS NETWORK

Pune: City-based Arogya Sena demanded that the Central Bureau of Investigation (CBI) look into the milk adulteration racket busted in Pune recently.

About 30 members of the Arogya Sena staged a protest outside the district collector's office on Friday and demanded that the names of dairy owners who were found involved in this racket should be announced.

Arogya Sena president Abhijit Vaidya said, "The administration has not disclosed the names of the dairy owners who were found guilty in this racket. The names will help the public as they will know that milk should not be bought from these particular dairy owners."

The members also burnt effigies of the three men who were arrested by the police in the milk adulteration racket.

The members met the collector and submitted their demands in writing to him.

The FDA will regularly inspect set-ups of milk producers and dairy owners to check if they are abiding by the rules and regulations, and check if the milk is being tested before it is sent to distributors and agencies. A similar meeting was held for milk producers in Sangli and Kolhapur in early September.

including item specific vessels, encouraging and developing deep sea fishing, setting up fisheries research institutes in each state and Union Territory, extension services for inland fish production, there is huge potential for growth of fisheries in the existing water resources.

Over and above existing water resources, if accelerated development is given to the artificial lakes creation, substantial additions to the canal length, river dredging and banking, joining of rivers etc., the fisheries sector has the potential to become a major food and nutrition giver to the citizens of India.

India exported in 2007-08, 541700 metric tons of fisheries at revenue of Rs. 7620 crore. There has to be long term policy of prohibiting export of fisheries also if real, truthful, all inclusive food guarantee for all the citizens of India is to be fulfilled.

Today's availability: 15 gm/capita/day.
Target: 50 gm/capita/day in 5 years.

Achieving the targets: There are many ways and means discussed here. Notwithstanding the same, good humungous planning and sincerity will deliver the results. In brief;

(i) For food self sufficiency, there is still opportunity though very brief one, to set long term policy goals and directions.

Panic driven short term solutions will only push the problem to near future again and in the process there is bound to be general public dissatisfaction, violence, retardation of growth, unemployment, hunger and poverty. Many years of hard work to uplift the living standards of the citizens' gets washed out in a year having 15% inflation of food items prices. Even by government method of defining poverty and the percentage below poverty line, suddenly the number of citizens getting pushed down under the poverty line become huge due to such inflation in food prices, that all calculations and projections become meaningless.

(ii) To invest substantially higher resources in productive capacity of agriculture and related areas than what has been the practice.

(iii) To do Pareto analysis and identify quick result areas and go after the same on war footing. As an example, for foodgrains, 80% of government procurement comes from north-west of India as a legacy of the green revolution of

1960s, now the emphasis and immediate investment could be in the north-east (eastern U.P., Bihar, West Bengal) to get substantial growth in foodgrains production.

Distribution: Every individual of our society/country has the fundamental right to get the above and the distribution mechanism is to be made of such good quality that all citizens are able to afford the above to fulfill their basic needs. To make this happen, fundamental requirements are:

(i) The government has to step in distribution of foodgrains and other food items at a colossally larger scale than it has been happening at present. Totally removing or marked reduction in intermediation in food market place is the only solution in the Indian context in the near future; to reduce price capture by intermediaries.

(ii) Improve the operation of food markets and distribution of wealth to actual growers of food.

(iii) Instead of wasting time and resources in determining who is poor, of what level of poverty and wasting resources in administrative controls in the distribution system; all citizens are to be considered and provided for. Since those who do not need assistance at present or who will not need in future (actually the number is going down due to traumatic inflation in prices of food items over the last few years), for some time to come, do form only a miniscule section of the Indian population.

(iv) Prices of food items have to be very low for all inclusive equitable distribution.

2. Clothes

At least one variety for men and one variety for women to be produced on very, very, very large scale and distributed at nominal payment/price (in many colours and prints).

This does not need explanation. It is feasible to do this item without much hassle and burden. The government should ensure distribution and quality besides the pricing. The distribution may be through enhanced Public Distribution System as well as all private and the government cloth material shops.

This production and availability is not to be limited only for citizens below poverty line. All citizens must be considered in planning without any differentiation in pricing. Those who do not need or will not buy, are not many in number at present scenario in the nation. Also the total resource requirement is much lower when it is for all due to simple administrative process.

Logic is to be extended in future for bed sheets and blankets for cold weather.

Target: 23 billion meter clothing material

@ price to citizens Rs. 2/ meter

3. *Home Building*

Plan and Implement large scale housing construction for housing to be made available to each and every household; and available at an affordable price.

There needs to be imaginative, large hearted, 'thinking big' planning for houses, flats or dwellings, focus being on improving the quality of standard of living of the citizens for long time to come. Buildings last for long periods and if the dwellings in these new buildings are with narrow thinking of profit and narrow mindset of poverty thinking; for long time to come, citizens of India will grow in these unlivable flats and houses.

The government have certain responsibilities in this direction.

(a) Legislation to be enacted that no new flat, house or dwelling is to be built, whether in urban or rural areas, having floor carpet area less than 100 sq. m (1000 sq. feet). This legislation is an urgent requirement considering the pigeon holes being built in India for human living. This legislation is to be enacted at central level and also at state levels and implemented earnestly.

Nobody will like the future generations of citizens to grow in poor and in physically and socially unhealthy environment. Every citizen has a right to live in decent dwelling, every child has a right to grow in decent dwelling and family environment. Cost of construction argument is meaningless at national level. At national level the dwellings are free.

If this legislation regarding minimum floor carpet area is passed, the future generations will really appreciate this generation for creating decent living environment. There will still be place in India for those who want to live in palaces or forts but if this is done the common man will not grudge the same.

(b) The price of a dwelling for a family is prohibitively high in urban areas; beyond reach of middle class families. This is bringing in loan culture of western nations in India too (we all should shy away), tempting people for financial frauds and criminal activities including murders. How a nation can be happy with such an environment? How its citizens can be happy and fearless?

And all this for nothing except for the benefit of some individuals and wrong national policy, rather specifically wrong national monetary policy.

Legislation is needed to correct this, fixing a rate which is affordable for a national median wage earner to own a house in 5 years. For a metro city, it could be the city median wage and for other city it has to be national median wage.

What really it means that the prices of land, real state, flats and houses have to be pushed significantly downwards by the governments for the benefit of the poor and the future generations. This in turn needs to push prices of construction materials downward, land is free at national level anyway and labour wages are for the purpose of distribution only.

(c) Quality of construction is to be maintained best as per latest technology. It costs nothing except seriousness, vision and diligence to maintain and enhance quality.

Target: to build 5000 townships of 300000 population capacity in 5 years; of minimum dwelling size of 100 sq. m/ house; @ price to citizens Rs. 1.8 lac/house.

4. Very large infrastructure projects to be implemented.

Creation of infrastructure is creation of long lasting wealth for a nation. As discussed earlier, on the national level, these do not need money for creation, only will power and very good methodology of distribution of food, housing, clothing and other essential goods are required.

Some of the large infrastructure projects are listed below. Action on some might have been initiated, some may be under consideration and many may be new; but the time is essence and the action to be at lightning speed to see the results.

Table 6: Infrastructure Development

	National assets (New creation)	5 - year target
1	Townships	5 000
2	Roads (Cement or paved metal km)	1000 000
3	Airports	6 000
4	Dredging of rivers (km)	100 000
5	Space satellites	100
6	Water canals (km)	100 0000
7	Artificial lakes	10 000
8	Connect rivers (connections)	100
9	Biodiversity sanctuaries/ parks	10 000
10	New railway lines (km)	100 000

11	Railway stations	3 000
12	Train bogies	30 000
13	School buildings	860 000
14	College buildings	135 000
15	University buildings/campuses	9 640
16	Vocational training centers	99 000
17	Underground shelters (Nuclear bomb protection)	10 000
18	Museums	2000
19	Stadiums	500
20	Aeroplanes	5 000
21	Fighter planes	10 000
22	Ships	5 000
23	Nuclear submarines	500
24	Battle tanks	50 000
25	Missiles	25 000
26	Super computers	1 000

We have all the above items in some measure, and more are being done. But the above targets seem to be insane. No! The above targets are achievable and the numbers are not big if we think of the size and the population of this county. We have 3280 000 sq. km. (3.28 million sq. km.) area of land, land borders with other countries 15200 km., coastline of 7500 km and 1200000000 (1.2 billion) population.

If we have to remove the poverty, we have to double or triple the numbers of some of the above items existing total quantity in the next 5 years. Some we have to create just in large numbers quickly. We have to increase the size or capability of each one of the above to meet the requirement and level to 100 years hence. We have to improve the quality of each of the above new creation to a level of the best in the world. The prime guru-mantra for removing poverty within 5 years is "TO THINK BIG". Whatever new is created, each one of the same is, will be, the biggest, best in the world now, in future and for the next 100 years to come. The power of scale has to be utilized while fixing the target.

Why only above items of infrastructure? (i) that are the final wealth items of use (ii) these are not intermediaries, intermediaries to be planned based on the above final products. (iii) the above list is having mixture of general public use and defence and technology items, (iv) for good planning and implementation focus must be kept on a few items only (v) the end returns or impacts on quality of living will be high and (vi) It will provide large employment opportunity with indigenous resources with least imports.

Townships

Every day huge number of people is moving to cities and towns. They come and form slums. Cities and towns attract humans due to safety instinct and instinct of living in groups. Life is more reassuring and probably convenient. Medical help is available. Employment or partial employment becomes available.

In India, from 1990 to 2000, 20.5 million people moved to urban areas of cities and towns. A conservative estimate predicts that 379 million people will be added to urban spaces over the next 40 years, more than the entire population of United States today.

Most of the mammals live in herds. Humans too wish to live in herds i.e. cities. It is part of inborn nature. Earlier most of the population used to live in villages though some part of population used to live in cities or towns.

Due to transformation in living conditions, electricity, telephone, transport etc., now all humans want to live in cities and towns. It is similar to pigeons living in the pigeon holes. At present, for very long time to come, this process of shifting towards and living in cities and townships is irreversible.

And hence create well planned, full of amenities, spacious peri-urban townships giving best living conditions for all. People will say money is required to do so. Sorry, money is only means of distribution and not creator of wealth like well planned townships. Only will-power is required at the national level. Planning to do this is required. Vision to do so is required. There is no lack of resources. Resources are available aplenty especially in India–the basic building materials, barren land, and the people to build.

An initial target is to be set for building 5000 peri-urban townships in 5 years capable of 300000 citizens habitation in each one of these. That is for a total 300000x 5000 = 1500000000 citizens (1.5 billion citizens). It is necessary to plan and create excess capacity for urban areas considering growth in population, people migrating from big cities to smaller cities and townships and of course people moving from rural to urban areas.

First planning is to be for the location of the townships. It should always be on large tract of barren, unsuitable for any activity for growing agriculture/fruit cultivation, fisheries or animal farms. This is to utilize available national land properly and usefully. Every state of India has such large tracts of barren land. Such lands are already identified, township locations need to be zeroed in on such lands.

Urban planning is required with essence of grandeur in thinking and with a motto of whatever will be provided will be the best, spacious and aesthetic.

Roads must be planned and developed in integrated form to have cables, water pipes, sanitary pipes, rainwater outlet pipes, water pipes for gardening of the plants in the middle, and on the sides of the footpaths, very, very wide footpaths for the citizens to have morning and evening walk must be considered. There must be gardens, entertainment centers, post-offices, banks, schools, universities, professional colleges, museums, biodiversity parks, zoo etc. as part of the planning and systematic implementations.

Transportation within the township for passengers and goods is to be considered as part of the planning. Planning time view to be 50 years at least, 100 years preferably.

Trees and floriculture are to be considered as part of the township building planning process and to be planted initially itself just after the surveying, marking of land, and allocating process is completed. Drawings of the township plans must show the landscaping also, including detail of long life trees to be planted. Building drawings must compulsorily show the landscaping for the building and the various trees' names and positions. Landscaping consultants must be as integral part of the architecture and engineers team. Trees and fruit trees having life of 100-200 years or more to be planted on the road sides and wherever space is available. Play gardens, schools, universities, professional colleges, entertainment centers museums to have medium life fruit trees besides lawns and flowers patches, because these plants normally enhance beauty due to colorful leaves and, bright flowers and colorful fruits.

A township for good living must be green all around. Human eyes, brain and body have special linkage to green leaves because when humans used to live in forests, lush green meant good food availability.

Last question on this will be who will come to live in a remote deserted place. Initially there will be many occupants in the cities for employment and gradually these will get saturated of people. If there is a university, professors and the administrative staff will live in the township. Their children will be in the schools. Teachers will be required in the schools.

Just like villages in ancient India used to be self-sufficient, self-sustaining; same way these townships are to be developed in such a fashion that these are self-sufficient and self sustaining.

Roads

Roads connect the cities, townships and villages for citizens to visit for their personal reasons.

However, roads serve another aspect i.e. security of a nation. Roads also connect for goods transportation.

The biggest purpose probably roads serve is bringing the concept of one Nation in the mind space of the citizens. Roads also help in administration of regions.

India needs to plan, and perfect the implementation process. Sometimes one gets feeling that our roads are planned by the people who have lived in poverty and miseries and small houses and small spaces.

A planner must first broaden his own viewpoints. That comes by exposure, richness feeling, and no-constraint resource availability.

Here we are not talking of in-city or in-township roads. The roads connecting the cities, township, villages have to be wide [at least 3 buses/trucks to move in one direction parallel to each other, +2 rows of cars in one direction], separate roads for the 2 directions of traffic. That is all new roads connecting township to be at least 10 lanes for the motor vehicles. There must be at least 2 lanes in each direction for bicycles. In the Indian conditions it is absolutely must to have bicycles lanes nicely done since villages are close by to each other and bicycles will remain and also must be encouraged as short distance transport system. It may be preferable to have motorcycles lanes also for up down of traffic, otherwise motorcycles will encroach in either the bicycles lanes or the motor vehicles lanes. This type of planning will also make driving safe.

Yes availability of land not taking away agricultural/forestry land will be a problem for building such wide roads.

Build roads over rivers; build multilevel roads—one way on the ground and other way over the same. Build multistory bus stands or truck stands. Build since it costs nothing, and keeps citizens employed in gainful activities. Build since it creates national wealth. Build since it creates infrastructure for increased human activities.

Target: To build 1 million km of roads (10+2+2 lanes) in 5 years and don't forget to plant long life trees to balance the CO_2 emission coming out of the vehicles on the roads. Each side to have at least two rows of long life trees.

Airports

Man has mastered the flying process probably as good as birds, actually better than birds since man while flying does nothing physical and flies in big groups. Flying is the best method of transport—time period taken to traverse is very less and hassle free. Only troublesome aspect is the aviation fuel. Who knows, tomorrow will be nuclear engines in the airplanes? And of course there will be more and more of personal flying machines.

Hence create big size, most modern airports in each city, townships and helipads in the villages. Build since it costs nothing. Build multilevel parking of aircrafts at the airports to save land use in the agricultural zone or food zone. Flying is not only present but future passenger/goods transport too. Build now, build fast. Build aesthetically. Build to last for 100 years to 500 years. If Taj Mahal can last for 400 years, why not airports build now last for 500 years.

There are only 130 airports in India. There are 19820 airports in USA out of which 600 are commercial airports for a population that is one fourth of India.

Target: To build 6000 new airports in 5 years.

Dredging of Rivers

Rainy season arrives, and floods arrive in India. People get displaced, crops are spoiled, animals and trees are killed. It is not rejuvenation by nature of the land, it is shame on humanity, and it is a shame on today's science and technical endeavour.

The above can easily be stopped by dredging of rivers that is making the river deeper and cleaning of the river bed.

This work should be taken up on large scale. With today's dredging machinery and earthmoving equipments, it is feasible and done quickly. What is needed for doing this is large scale production of these equipments and planning to implement this river operation for all the rivers.

Whereever a river passes through a city, a township or a village, build the river of cement bed and cement banks so that yearly cleaning will let the water pass through smoothly. Obviously the banks to be high enough and river bed to be wide enough to take water flow of rainy season and double triple margin i.e. thrice the amount of water can flow than what is there in normal rainy season.

Target: Every river in India will be made 2 meters deeper at all the place from its current river bed height from sea level. 100 000 km lenght to be completed in 5 years.

Construction of River Banks

Building river banks on both sides of the river is discussed just earlier. Let the imagination fly. The banks are to be made high and create road over the banks as side walls. Make long river fly-overs. This way, land procurement hassles will be reduced.

This will need development of technology and its perfection to get long life. And if this is done, the fisheries production could be increased multifold by water banking in the rivers.

Mechanizing of the fish catching could be designed and implemented at certain length intervals of the rivers. The earth material which gets removed while dredging forms normal enhanced river banks if done properly.

Target: 100 000 km of river banks in 5 years and 150 000 km. road over river banks.

Space Satellites

Satellites in space have become commonplace. Its utility is great and power to change life and society is unquestionable. Satellite phones do not need cables or towers. Satellite beams back the TV programmes what is watched in the homes.

Satellite cameras take photos which are used for security and for weather conditions.

So increase the number of satellites put by India in space dramatically. It is national wealth in space. The cost of satellite is nil at national level because all parts are made in India; but benefits are great, wide ranging and many times over. There are many categories of satellites for serving specific services.

Target: Total number of new satellites put by India to be 1000 in 5 years.

Water Canals

In a nation of India size and climate, canals are lifelines just like arteries in the body. These provide water in those areas which are not close to rivers. Canals are nothing but rivers made by humans.

To make canals, we do not need to import anything. There are powerful digging and earthmoving equipments which create canals at a rapid speed. Even cementing/brick or plastic application of the canal bed and side banks could be mechanized.

Canals to be created along the new roads since earth dug for making the canal to be used for making raised road and leveling of the roads by the sides of the canals. Canal and road development are to be integrated.

Railway track lines have wide space on both sides of the lines. Both extreme sides could be used for creating narrow but very long canals. That will help the farmers along the railway property and also for making the railway empty property green all along.

The benefits of getting water through canals do not need any elaboration. Food security alone demands mammoth work plan to build canals all over the nation.

Target: To build 100 000 km additional length of canals in India in the next 5 years

Artificial Lakes

India is a blessed country that it has enviable percentage of its land as arable. However land use for agriculture, fruit cultivation, and raising of animals, can be substantially enhanced by creating artificial lakes in the dry arid reasons.

As discussed earlier, lakes are to be created preferably at the foot hills so that the hill works as catchment area for the lakes. Most of the hills have sloped foot hill.

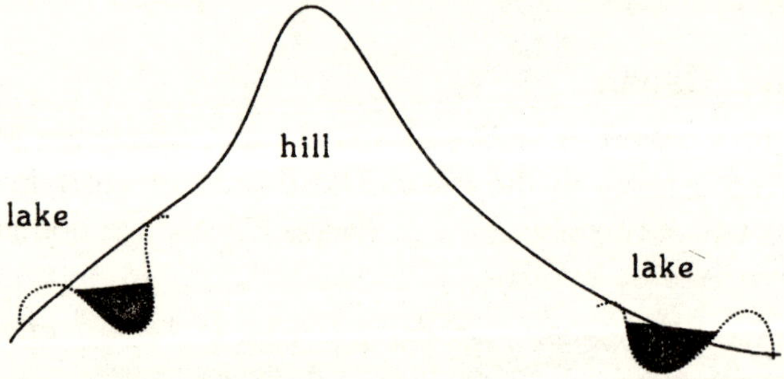

It is easy to create a lake as shown in the diagram above. It is blasting and removal of the earth using earthmoving equipments—shovels, dozers, backhoes, etc. Spreading plastic sheets created for this purpose with suitable sealed joining at the base will make water last longer. Some plastic materials permeate/dissolve in water though at a very slow rate but could prove fatal/harmful to humans and animals over a period of time; such plastic materials must not be used for lining of the lake.

The whole process could be mechanized to a great extent. To make a medium size lake, it may not take more than 1–3 months depending on the terrain. Standardize the sizes of lakes as given below.

- 70 meters wide X 300 meters long X 10 meters deep
- 100 meters wide X 500 meters long X 10 meters deep
- 150 meters wide X 800 meters long X 15 meters deep
- 200 meters wide X 1000 meters long X 20 meters deep

The lakes are to be made in less rain fed areas, hilly or plain.

While making a lake, pipe connection with valves also to be fixed so that controlled water discharge can be made at will.

Target: To create 10000 artificial lakes in the next 5 years.

Connect the Rivers

The process is making canals joining two rivers so that water flow in the rivers becomes amenable to control. Also canal gives its own benefit where it passes on.

The map shows just indicative joining points for major river systems. Plan and build since it costs nothing at the national level. Joining the rivers does not need anything to import. It needs powerful earthmoving equipments and sand and cement.

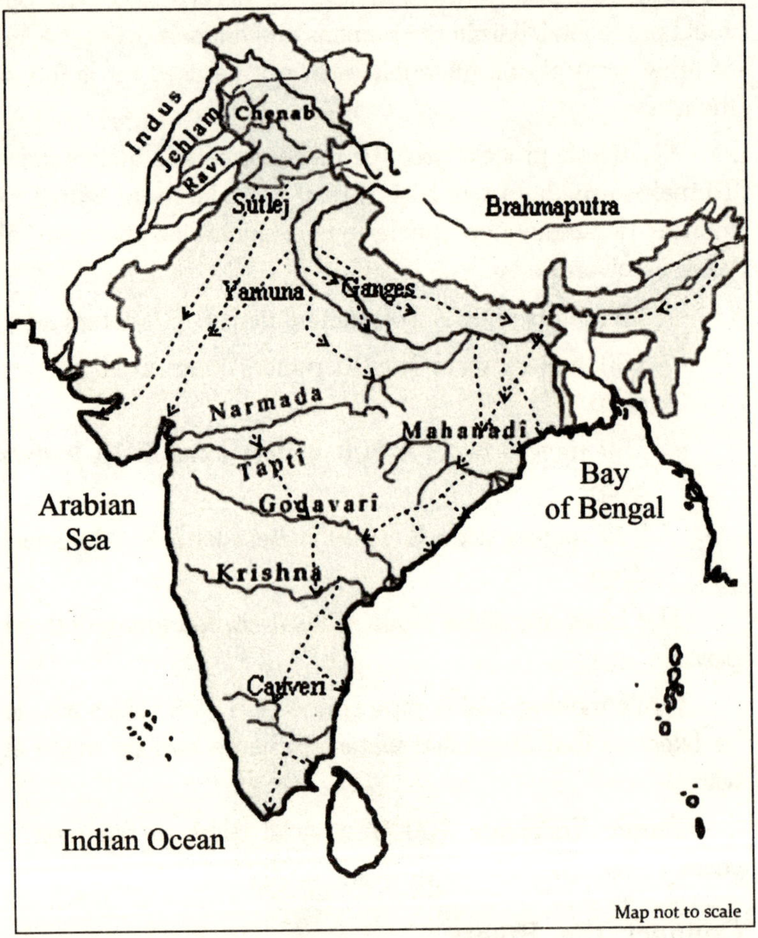

The canals joining the river systems are to be very deep and narrow so as to take minimum land.

It is obvious that joining should always be at the downstream of one river to the upstream of another river to get the natural flow of water. There is no point in connecting upstream to upstream since there may not be enough water to flow. The decision to joining of rivers is to be made quickly because beyond this consideration, all other aspects are secondary and of logistics in nature which could be sorted out later in the programme. There is no point in delaying for 50 years debating its worthiness or availability of resources.

Logic of joining of the rivers in the attached map is the following.

(a) Punjab and West UP rivers are interconnected and water is brought to Gujarat through Punjab, Haryana and Rajasthan.

(b) Ganga is connected to Yamuna somewhere in west UP to have control on water flow quantity based on glaciers melting rate in the Himalayas.

(c) A canal more or less parallel to Ganga is created joining various tributaries through Uttarakhand meeting Ghagra for the reasons of balancing the water in Ganga and also in other tributaries and further east meeting downstream Ganga.

(d) Creating a parallel Brahmaputra through Indian territories and meeting Ganga and many of tributaries and other rivers in Jharkhand and West Bengal.

(e) Joining Chamba through various tributaries of Yamuna and Ganga to balance water availability throughout the year and is to be parallel to Yamuna, joining Ganga downstream.

(f) On the east coast creation of many sub-river systems meeting the sea. It is not necessary that water has to flow to the sea all the time.

(g) Joining tributaries and rivers in central and south India.

Target: A minimum programme of rivers joining canals shown in the map to be implemented in 5 years.

New Railway Lines

India is a vast country, to cover and provide rapid transportation from one township to another township nearby or far away, the rail connection is just beautiful, convenient if frequency is appropriate and it is not crowded, and if one needs not get it reserved months in advance.

At present rail travel in India is not beautiful, mostly it is punishment. To take care of the needs of the prosperous population, there have to be more trains, frequent trains and enough time available for track maintenance and bogies maintenance.

Rail is also vital for goods transportation. Creating more railway lines and more bogies is creating national wealth, and also strengthening of the infrastructure.

Both goods and passenger bogies are to be made lighter. There is tremendous scope for reduction of weight of the bogies—both passenger and goods. Using modern tools of stress and deflection analysis, the bogies' weights can be reduced substantially without affecting the life or safety. The weight reduction of bogies will give ample saving of fuel or electricity. Inside portion of the bogies of passenger trains must be made of stainless steel. Besides enhancing the aesthetic look, it will help in maintaining cleanliness and will give much longer bogie life. And at national level it costs nothing because stainless steel is produced within the nation's boundaries using available natural resources.

There is tremendous scope to increase aesthetics, functional requirements, cleanliness by design and more amenities in the passenger bogies. Railways must wake up and do commendable work on these before mass production of standardized bogies to be taken up in future.

Creating railway lines needs nothing to import and it is free at the national level. India has total railways route length of 63221 km for 1200 million citizens. The USA has 226612 km railway line for 303 million people, Russia has 87157 km length railway line for just 141 million citizens.

India has to create 14 times more of existing length of railway line to match USA and 12 times to match Russian facility. So build it for transportation, build for prosperity, build for safety and build for the nation's wealth.

Length of Railway Line/Citizen

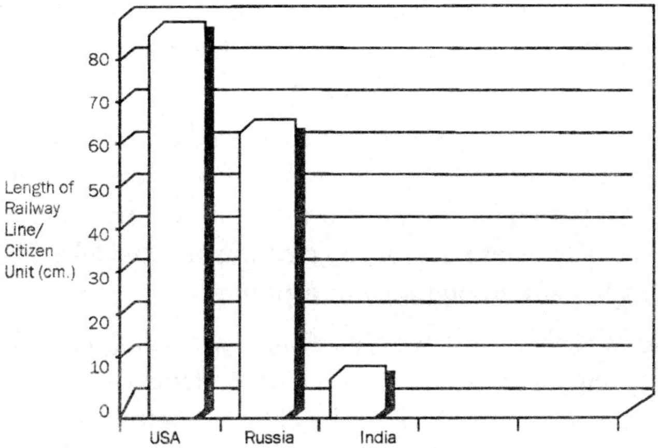

Target: To triple the network of railway lines in 5 years or 100000 km of new railway lines to be created in 5 years.

Create Biodiversity Parks

Nature on this earth has created very big pool of life forms. India being a tropical country and having very diverse climate of extreme cold to extreme hot conditions, deserts to highly fertile land, different conditions of rains and long land sea interface, is a blessed country for biodiversity.

India has unmatched diversity of trees, plants, weeds, flowers, fruits, animals, birds, insects, reptiles, etc. and India must preserve this nature's gift to all the Indians and to the world.

These species are priceless and must live as Indians live. But sadly many species are disappearing, for most of the species the population numbers are dwindling at a very fast rate, because of the human activities, nay unplanned human activities.

If human activities are done in a planned fashion, planning done by visionaries, balance of various life forms could be maintained.

The governments should declare all the existing forests as sanctuaries or biodiversity parks. The small patches of forest lands as sanctuaries and that also only a few numbers is no justice to our contemporary life forms.

Not only all existing forests to be declared as "biodiversity parks" and documented and protected; new ones must get created. The barren lands must be the basis for the creation of new ones--by planting trees, by creating artificial lakes, by creating high walls around for protection.

Besides replicating India's biodiversity, small patches of completely enclosed and sealed bio diversity sanctuaries duplicating world's other regions by climate controls must be created in every city and townships; for the knowledge of young and old; for research by universities and professional colleges teaching biology, botany, sociology, psychology, entomology and environment subjects.

Build since it costs nothing. Build for the pleasure of human eyes. Build for the pleasure of eyes of the citizens. Build for research. Build for the children. Build for the future generations.

Machinery, technology and process to plant trees even in rocks need to be looked at. A big size tree will grow and sustain in a two meters diameter, two meters deep pit filled with earth and manure. With modern technology the whole process of planting trees in rocky terrain could be a mechanized process for quick and lasting results. Similarly develop technologies of climate control for large enclosures with transparent tops and sides for sunlight. Other countries have such enclosed climate controlled large size biodiversity parks. Let us make even bigger than the big ones.

Target:
(a) To create 5000 biodiversity parks of at least 20 sq. km. each.

(b) To create 5000 small patches (2-5 acres) of climate controlled bio diversity parks in/

nearby every city and township. Every city or town to have at least one climate controlled biodiversity park.

5. Production

Production of goods using available natural resources, intermediate goods and manpower creates wealth in a nation.

India is a big country with plenty of natural resources both renewable and non-renewable types. Manpower is in abundance available, so goods should be produced on large scale for intermediate use in industry and for final consumption by citizens.

Goods needed for primary production and consumption of food, house-building, clothing and items needed for creating very large infrastructure must get priority for development and encouragement by properly directing through monetary policy. Many of the intermediate goods needed in these sectors also must be part of the primary development plan, example; power, steel, fertilizers, cement, big trucks, small trucks, earthmoving equipments, mobiles, computers etc., etc.

Then there should be secondary production items; cars, costly goods for luxurious living or life style differentiating goods, expensive furniture, rather every item for end use consumption for differentiating individual status or wealth.

The governments must not ever venture, subsidize, encourage these industries of secondary production items under any pressure or false lure of employment creation. These should be left to the capitalist and democratic processes and the development of such industries is to be market dependent and governed by pure market forces.

Cigarettes, alcohols and dependency on drugs are to be discouraged and regulated.

Primary goods production and pricing are to be regulated by governments keeping proper distribution in mind. The prices of primary goods have to be low and the industries in this category must have stable production rate with good quality. These industries must be expanded at very high rate by encouraging, subsidizing, and assuring of end consumption by the governments.

It is not necessary that these primary goods industries have to run only by the governments. No, not at all, these industries may have private organizations, may have government organizations, and may have government and private mixed organizations. But these industries must have greater government controls to initially driving down the prices artificially. This process will increase the intrinsic value of the national currency over a period of time.

For these primary goods production profits are to be minimal and any excessive profiteering by individuals must be dealt very harshly (5 to 7% of profit on sales turnover is normally good in industry). In these industries salaries are to be kept low and the difference from lowest to the highest is also to be minimal. These industries employment is to be looked upon primarily as distribution of primary goods to larger population. Politics is not to play or play very little role in these industries.

Secondary goods markets and the market players must have complete freedom. The dance of democracy, the dance of capitalism, the dance of personal wealth creation and destruction, the dance of happiness and unhappiness, the dance of Shiva happens in this arena. In these industries people may satisfy their aspirations, their craze, their courage, their ambitions, their ruthlessness, etc., to the highest possible pitch.

The governments should generate good revenues from the secondary goods production and consumption. This is the revenue from which the governments run and production of primary goods is to be subsidized.

The vice goods or "harmful to humans" goods production will need discouragement. The revenue from these goods is to be classified and treated "toxic revenue" and targets to be fixed for reduction of such revenues; but such industries and consumers need to pay taxes at the highest level. It will be argued that this will lead to black marketing and unlawful trade if demand exists. Actually these toxic revenues to be utilized in creating awareness and training and persuasion to reduce the end consumer demand. Instead of increased spending on health care; it is better not to have these revenues or have to the minimal.

6. Defence

Defence employs (keeps engaged) number of citizens directly and a good number indirectly.

There are articles advocating reduction in defence budget and there are articles advocating increase in defence budget. It is like "c" or "s" in the spelling of defence.

It is not fundamentally correct that when there are so many poor in India, why spend on defence or defence expenditure must be curtailed. But actually the expenditure in itself on defence has nothing to do with poverty, or rather this expenditure is necessary and to be enhanced to remove poverty.

What is wrong is the import content of the defence expenditure. That is giving away the resources and the hard work of people of India to the countries from where imports come. At present this import content of defence is humungous; 70% of the total expenditure on procurement of capital acquisition.

In favour of imports, it is argued that technology is not available within the country. It is fallacious arguments by those who are interested in the import deals for some other extraneous factors. Instead of importing 100 Bofors guns, if resources used for one gun procurement would have been used appropriately, and at right time; an Indian gun would have got developed with similar or better features. If price for one gun paid in dollar term is "X" then actual resources used of the country is "5X" due to the exchange rate distortion. Also once the gun would have got designed and developed with local material; India would not have hundred but 10000 of those guns with the same resource utilization. Multiplication factor is not only 5 but 100 because of huge profit margins on these imports charged by the exporting organizations. All the people who have been associated with such sales understand it fully.

The other argument in favour of imports is put that the equipments developed in India do not perform. Do the equipments developed abroad and supplied to us do not fail or under perform? Take example of MIG 21 fighters imported from abroad, every other day newspapers carry report of crash of a MIG fighter.

The one more argument put forward by promoters of imports of defence equipments is the time factor or operational exigencies. The country has to be prepared now for the new strategic scenario and development of the equipment will take too much of time which the country can hardly afford. But can't we sit and plan defence capability requirements for the next year, next 5 years, next 10 years, next 15 years, next 20 years and 30, 40, 50 years. In that case there will be ample time available for indigenous developments. This is exactly what those exporting countries are doing; they offer to sell to us not their latest technology but the obsolete technology in the name of it being better than what they sold to our neighbour. This exercise of long term planning in advance and earmarking different agencies public and/or private to deliver will reduce the imports to a great extent if not totally eliminate.

And it does not mean that all imported equipments under-perform or fail. Similarly it does not mean that all India developed equipments fail or underperform. Design and development of any type of equipment is always progressive in nature that is the design quality, manufacturing quality, features up-gradation, new generations etc., are always based on experience. If opportunity of this type is not given to the Indian firms by ordering and using, we will never, never get out of this colonial mindset.

It is true that due to the imports in defence, there is no chance for local development. Any equipment design undergoes improvements as the equipments are used.

There is one point which is ignored at present while considering defence imports of fighters, submarines, intelligence equipments, etc. The spying gadgets are fitted on the imported equipments. Today's, electronics is highly sophisticated and most of the defence equipments have electrical and electronic contents. The supplier countries of these equipments are mostly developed countries and it is not in their interest to make us strong. These countries will not be skipping the lure of putting highly sophisticated spy content on the export of the equipment on high moral ground of ethics. The purchaser may think smart that checks are feasible but anybody familiar with telecom, satellite and electronics new developments, knows the difficulty in detection and the high degree of possibility of not getting the detection. In that case all the strategies and actions of the purchaser country get passed to the supplier country. How one can win a war in such a case?

Ethics or ethical behaviour is a talk for others i.e. for other countries, especially in the western civilization. If ethical behaviour was the prime guiding factor—Red Indians would not have got wiped out from American mainland, India would not have been under British rule for 200 years, Soviet Union would not have broken up, and India would not have been divided in two, India and Pakistan. There are innumerable examples from recent history too or even from contemporary history.

If ethics was considered, the United Nations would have had Hindi also as official language. Currently official languages of U.N. are Arabic, Chinese, English, French, Russian and Spanish. As first language, Arabic is spoken by 280 million, English by 375 million, French by 77 million, Russian by 160 million, similarly Spanish by a few million persons in the world. As first language, Hindi is spoken by 450 million persons in the world and as second language additional 400 million persons speak Hindi. But Hindi is not an official language of United Nations.

If ethics was considered, why India is not a permanent member of the UN Security Council? Following is the number of persons India represents compared to the number of humans the permanent Security Council members represent.

UN Official languages—Spoken population size (in million)

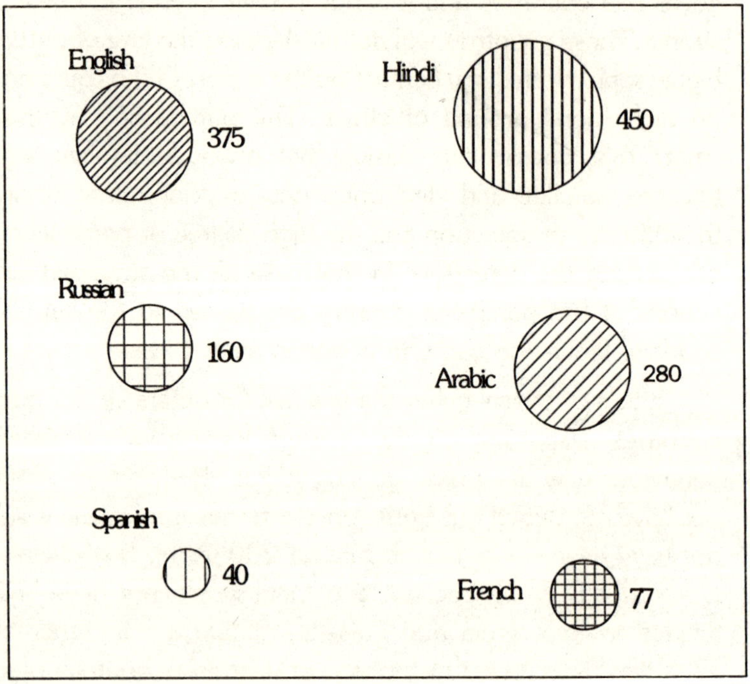

Table 7: UN Security Council Permanent Members

Country	Country Population (million)	% of India Population	% of World Population
USA	304	25 (1/4th.)	4.5
UK	61	5 (1/20th.)	0.91
FRANCE	62	5 (1/20th.)	0.92
RUSSIA	141	12 (1/8th.)	2.1
CHINA	1330	111	19.8
INDIA (not a member)	1200		17.9
WORLD	6710		

Four out of five permanent members of the United Nations Security Council are representing a miniscule percentage of world population whereas India representing much bigger percentage of world population is not a permanent member yet. Those who used violence and looted earlier, want continuation of power to make the policies for the security of all the citizens of the world.

If ethics was the guiding factor, why India was considered apartheid for developing nuclear technology whether for peaceful purposes or for defence purposes?

UNSC Permanent Members' Country Population (India not member)

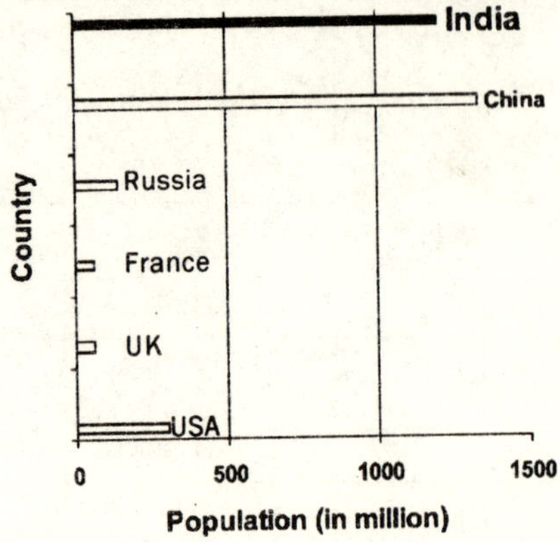

UNSC Permanent members population (percentage of world population)

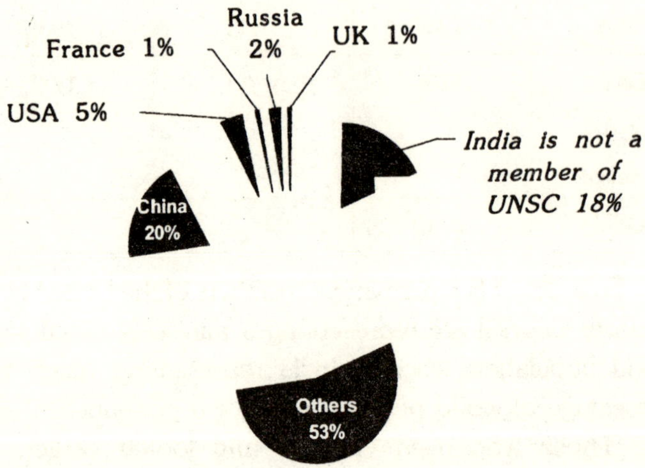

India as a country has to be extraordinarily careful because of the psyche difference. The psyche difference comes due to weather conditions and long historical reasons. Just imagine 6 persons in Germany left for a year in an area 400 years ago. The area was far away from settlements. After an year only one or two will be surviving. They would have died due to non availability of food in that iceland of long winter or killed by treachery of the surviving members to corner whatever food becomes available or to eat the meat of the weak fellow men. Take six people in India and leave them away from settlements 400 years ago, same time period. For most part of India (probably except Himalayas or deserts of Rajasthan) chances were that all the six would have survived the year by eating fruits, animal meat, or roots etc. If anyone would have died, chances are it would have been due to disease or snake bite or killed by animal.

The general Indian psyche is "Live and Let Live". The harsh climate (mostly very cold) countries have the psyche "Survival of the Fittest". There is nothing wrong with any of this psyche because both come from the immediate natural environment and on food availability. Just like nothing wrong with cows and lions both are nature's creations. But the dealings between the two could be disastrous. The person with "Live and Let Live" psyche has more probability of getting eliminated or suppressed by the person having psyche of "Survival of the Fittest" .The person with psyche of "Live and Let Live" has to be extra careful and use human canny to survive in such a situation. Since people make nations, it is true for nations too.

So extra resources, efforts and planning are to be put and that will technologically leap-frog on defence capabilities. Develop all equipments (needed by defence) inside the country. Develop inside the country all equipments required by defence plan of 5 years, 10 years, 15 years, 20 years, 30, 40, 50 years. Initiate big development R&D programmes now and use the equipments developed out of R&D efforts. Development of future equipments initiated today has to be priority, and R&D is free at national level. Manpower is available; use the same to develop technologies for defence of the country.

Methodically, any political party which sanctions imports beyond a meager 2 or 3% of the total defence budget should be voted out in elections, because it is not working in the interest of the country, and that also in a sensitive area of national security. If Israel (having population of 7.5 million only) could develop all types of sea, air and land based highly technically advanced defence systems, if UK (having population of 61 million only) could do the same, if USA (having population of 304 million only) could do the same, if France (having population of 62 million only) could do the same, if Canada (having population of 33 million only) could do the same; why not India (having population of 1200 million) can do the same. The countries listed below only export defence equipments and their own imports of defence equipments are either negligible or part of collaborative arrangements with each other.

Table 8: Import/Export of Defence Equipment

Country	Population	Export		Import	
	(Million)	(Billion)		(Billion)	
		US$	Rs.	US$	Rs.
USA #	304	32	1540		
UK #	61	10	480		
Russia#	141	11	530		
France#	62	2	95		
Israel	7.5	0.5	24		
Canada	33	1	45	0*	0*
India	**1200**	0	0	10	480

The above explanation has driven the point that large expenditure on defence is essential, and helpful to remove the poverty as long as it remains and emphasizes the local content.

USA, UK, Russia, Germany and France accounted for about 80% of total arms exports in the year 2007.

* The net import is zero, since as per IRB programme of Canada; winning contractors are required to make investments in advanced technology sectors of the Canadian economy in an amount equal to the contract value.

Technology development in defence and defence equipments is required to be at the cutting edge, highly sophisticated and in some areas highly futuristic. Let resources be put on this Research and Development.

'Make' procedure of defence ministry of India started recently is a step in the right direction. This procedure is to ensure indigenous research, design, development and production capabilities sought by the armed forces in a time frame while utilizing the potential of Indian industry. But highly aggressive approach to this end with emphasis on quality of personnel, freedom to think, daring allotment of resources, fixing of dream targets, managerial restructuring and imaginative planning are required to achieve the end of self sufficiency.

Future warfare can only be won, (if won by anybody) based on Space Technology. This field must be given long term boost, besides all other cutting edge technologies defence needs or will need.

Target: (a) Increase the resource allocation to defence 100%, but increase to be in technology and local development.

(b) Imports in Defence sector not to increase 2% of total defence budget, to be gradually achieved in the coming 5 years. This is to be achieved taking into consideration the operational and strategic exigencies.

(c) To place orders on local organizations to develop, manufacture and supply (with 98% indigenous content) in 5 years: Space Satellites-500 nos., Missiles-25000 nos., Transport Planes-3000 nos., Fighter Planes-10000 nos., Ships - 2500 nos., Nuclear Submarines-500 nos., Battle Tanks-50000 nos., Super Computers - 200 nos.

The above numbers are not big, just to give an example Russia has got 80000 land systems (battle tanks) compared to India having only 10000. A small country like North Korea has 97 submarines.

7. Research And Development

R&D is free at the national level.

Once a nation has produced all the food it needs, all the clothing people need, all the housing it requires and also produced all the life style or status differentiating goods and services; and still has excess manpower, put them in R&D.

The nation has to still feed, clothe and house these (excess in numbers) citizens and instead of keeping this number of its citizens idle, put them in R&D. In R&D these people will develop engineering, science and technology aspects which will refine/create new goods, processes and services. These people serve a nation in a way to keep a nation going, self-sustaining and progressing ahead. Hence these numbers of people are not excess numbers but a necessary resource. The countries which have already produced/made available food and clothing and housing consider and do import people from other countries to work in R&D.

And R&D is free at the national level since anyway nation would have provided basic needs fulfillment. The salary or expenditure on R&D personnel is only to have distribution of goods and services process going on or as a media of distribution. The land, the building, and the equipments etc. used in this endeavour of R&D are available at the national level if it is from within the nation. If there are imported contents (and to some extent it must be there to keep the windows open for learning) seminars and visits abroad (very necessary for ideas), the resources required for these activities are to be balanced by the exports just like other necessary imports need to be balanced by exports.

Culture of R&D in each and every area of human requirement and environment to be fostered, encouraged, supported and results used on national/local basis. Every field of human endeavour must have R&D work attached to it, made part of the process, created as part of the establishment.

It looks funny but if a nation has to remove poverty, create R&D section even in zoos, for each agricultural crop, for each fruit variety, for urban housing, for clothing, for each animal specie, for each tree specie, for each insect specie, for each bird specie, for each body part, for each feeling of human beings besides industries having R&D for products and goods.

India has manpower as resource and even after use of necessary manpower for all the production, services required at national level; substantial manpower is/will be available for deploying in R&D. Creation of research & development section everywhere, every location like a maniac is not only absolutely necessary for survival in the modern world; but for removing poverty.

The persons in R&D need certain personality attributes of analysis and synthesis. These are not in-born qualities. These come by training of mind and thoroughness depends on the use of training, quality of training and level of intelligence of the individual. Those with higher educational degrees, those with higher IQs (example beyond 130) irrespective of the educational level, are to be deployed in R&D activities. Training and exposure of these individuals must be of the highest standard.

The above will not be a favour to the individual or a profession; it is a favour to the future generation of the citizens of the country.

Some R&D Projects @ National Level

This list below is not exhaustive but exotic enough with great potential benefits. Some might be being worked upon in India too.

(a) Developing a plane, or a flying saucer or a device to travel in space and carry a payload of at least 2 tons. The device should be re-usable i.e. it should return back at the place of choice.

(b) Setting a manned base on the moon. Target 10 manned bases in the next 5 years.

(c) Development of satellites which continuously take photos/monitors every inch of the borders and 1000 km beyond borders and send the information on real time basis.

The resolution of the monitoring is to be such that even if a rabbit moves, it gets recorded with clarity that it is a rabbit.

(d) Bases in Antarctica: Target year round 10 bases with 100 men each. Food grown on site.

(e) Miniature nuclear reaction powered engine running on water as fuel; for use in air, surface and sea transportation. Target in 5 years.

(f) Setting up base of 100 men at the bottom of the sea. Target 100 bases in 5 years along the Indian coast. Food production on site.

(g) Develop robot soldier with automatic firing abilities and for monitoring of the borders. Design to be conducive for mass production. Time target: 5 years.

(h) Develop material which has specific gravity of 0.5 gm./cc but is tougher and harder than steel. The constituents to be abundantly available materials inside the country. If it will be so light then think of the benefit to the nation in terms of energy saving in transportation.

(i) Electric power transmission without use of cables.

(j) If another country fires a missile, the missile to be destroyed within 5-10 seconds of its firing i.e. a high speed missile to strike the enemy missile automatically either fired from surface or from space. Alternatively, the enemy missile is to be destroyed using electric power, laser power, or possibly photon power; but the speed of travel has to be close to the speed of light.

(k) To develop personal flying contraption. A human must be able to fly just like a bird.

(l) To develop wheat, rice and pulses plants which produce seeds within one month after sowing. This will be next green revolution.

(m) To develop nuclear powered missile with a range of 25000 km and accuracy of one meter and payload capacity of 2 tons.

(n) To develop brain cells using stem cells, the brain cells to be used in super computers – of course with nutrients supply system.

(o) To develop skin cells using stem cells. The skin to be bullet proof and to be used for producing second skin clothing on humans.

In General

There are many aspects which could be thought of or argued upon that those are also essential to remove poverty. But it is not being considered here to keep focus. A restricted focus is necessary for good planning and implementation of any programme. That is true for war on poverty too.

If the basic framework which is enumerated here in this book is followed and worked upon with zeal of war; the physical poverty will disappear from India. Once the physical poverty disappears, the other forms of poverty will automatically reduce to minimal. For example, psychological or social poverty cannot be eliminated totally. Hey! But it is feasible, possible, and achievable to remove physical poverty completely in a time frame of 5 years.

The governments should attempt to work on this plan sincerely and result will be visible in a very short time of 2 years.

The Planning Process

This is the backbone of the programme of 100% poverty removal in 5 years.

It needs a team of experts and non-experts (for no-set eyes) to be housed in one place. The team need not and should not be too big and too small. Maybe 50 committed persons team (no secretaries please) will be ok. The bureaucrats or industrial managers or politicians are not to be placed in this apex team.

Well groomed, well educated, out of box thinkers, believers and committed individuals will be the best choice to be in the team. No one individual heads the total team. Five persons form an apex planning team or as the war-room members, to guide and monitor the work.

The process of planning will also need strategizing for implementation portion.

Really planning for 100% removal of poverty is nothing but setting targets in the limited areas as indicated in this book and then detailing of the targets on geographical/unit basis and finally putting strategy for the implementation. Apex co-ordination on the actual implementation and dynamically modifying/adjusting the targets breakup will be the main work over a period of time.

The Implementation Machinery

Whenever it was mentioned that it is feasible to remove poverty within 5 years to a group, the first reaction was – it is a joke. When explained the concept properly, then the exclamation was; it is feasible in principle but implementation is not feasible, will not be implemented, our politicians cannot implement, corruption will not let it happen, etc, etc.

It is doable, feasible, and implementable easily. What is needed is the will to implement at the highest levels. When

Vajpayee as PM of India wished in year 2003 to join the metros in India by at least 4 lane highways; everybody doubted the same. There was an editorial in *The Times of India* at that time that Vajpayee is out of his mind, where from 64000 crore rupees will come to build those roads. But he insisted and lo! it happened in five years' time.

As explained umpteen numbers of times in this book, that resources are no constraints in India; rupees or money is not required for doing this. What is needed is will at the highest levels, planning and sincere implementation. Corruption is not a hindrance in removing the poverty at the national level. Corruption of an individual to getting more money, more houses, more cars etc. is meaningless at the national level. It is like a man having 10 diamonds, instead of one entitlement each. The person will still eat only what he can eat, he will wear clothes only, may be along with jewellery which are just small amounts of metals and stones, he will use many cars which are just 300 kg to 200 kg. of steel and some other material. At national level 200 kg. of steel will cost Rs. 80000 only at current prices.

So corruption is no hindrance in removing poverty. It is not that corruption should be encouraged; it is mentally and socially a plague. But for removing physical poverty, this aspect could be ignored to maintain focus.

Similarly, money stacked in foreign banks by some individuals is of no consequence in removal of physical poverty.

If the central government and state governments unanimously decide to focus and follow the principles and programmes as explained in this book, physical poverty will disappear in 5 years. Skeptics will say even in America 10% of people live below poverty line, how India can eliminate 100% poverty.

What is enumerated in this book, if America will follow (they do follow to some extent), remaining 10% poverty will disappear in their country too. Implementation of these programmes does not need great changes in the structure of the governments. No, really no changes are required in the structure.

The central planning team have to make plans and communicate and train the ministries personnel, with an advice on procedure of implementation and targets for implementation.

Now, ministries have to be efficient, determined, with focus on communication and training. Targets must be met at all levels, targets have to be ambitious. Performance appraisal with reward and punishment may be there, albeit that is not the crux or critical. Crux is the emotional, motivational, patriotic uprising of the government machinery to implement. A good government and good governance requires imbibing the above qualities for efficiency, enthusiasm and results.

Summary

- *Setting up big targets and enthusiasm to meet the same is the direction to follow for a nation too, just like in industry.*
- *No targets are unrealistic or unachievable.*
- *Exports of essential goods like food, clothing and inputs for production of food, clothing and shelter to be banned for long period, say 20 years.*
- *Governance of equitable distribution system to be achieved by monetary policy.*
- *For the first 5 years of total removal of poverty programme, the wealth items and the targets to be planned and implemented without discussion, to achieve quick results. All discussions to happen in the 5th year to include new wealth items for the*

next 5 years and any course corrections for the next 50 years.

With democratic setup of governance, it is feasible to remove physical poverty in 5 years even in a country like India, which has over 50% of population poor. The senior honest politicians and bureaucrats have to make the determination to do the same. It costs nothing, they loose nothing. Nation's gain is enormous.

Chapter - 11

MONETARY POLICY

I saw the best minds of my generation destroyed by madness, starving, hysterical naked...

— Allen Ginsberg, Howl

In this global world and era of awareness, old tools of change—patriotism, moral authority, profit a bad word, coercion, call for decent values, etc., do not catch the imagination of citizens. The governance has become giving direction by monetary policies.

In a democracy, private enterprises need to be encouraged intentionally to let each and every person does his/her best for the society while doing best for self psychologically, intellectually, physically and socially.

Having said the above, further analysis is necessary. Every citizen is a human being and equal in a democracy. Every human being is equal in principle, should be treated equal by a democratic government, is supposed to be equal in the eyes of judiciary due to moral reasons, owns the earth equally along with other contemporary human beings and hence has equal rights.

Having said the above, further analysis and perception is necessary. All the above is only in principle, should be etc., etc. But in reality, (i) all human beings are not made equal mentally; (ii) all human beings are not created equal physically, (iii) all human beings do not have same stamina and strength, (iv) and due to these 3 reasons, are not born with equal resources of their parents/near relatives.

Having said the above, further analysis, perception and realism is necessary. Though every child, when born, is born free, owns the earth and its resources the same way as any other new-born baby; but in reality it does not happen so, is not true and probably can never be made true (even by communism) fully.

Having said the above and besides analysis, perception, realism; understanding is also necessary. It is easy to say that let the fit ones only survive, let only capable ones survive, let only strong survive. But then that will not be the foundation stone of society, that will be breaking a main pillar of a nation. Not only, it will be even bad democracy.

Having said the above and besides analysis, perception, realism, understanding; empathy is necessary for a good society, for building an all inclusive nation, for creating foundation of a durable national character and strong nation with democratic traditions.

Having said the above, and besides analysis, perception, realism, understanding, empathy; methodical plans are necessary to do the all inclusive development and remove poverty totally. Since, money is the means of distribution, monetary policy determines who gets what when distributed. Monetary policy is like a guiding system of a missile; money or monetary policy is not the ammunition, is not the missile but it is the guiding system which determines how accurate and where the ammunition is delivered. An imaginative monetary policy, with dynamic feedback, control and corrective mechanism will go a long way and in very speedy removal of poverty.

Having said the above, and besides analysis, perception, realism, understanding, empathy, methodical plans of monetary policy; a ruthless implementation, nay a speedy implementation of the determined monetary policy is necessary for proper distribution of the goods and services. Even if sufficient quantity of goods and services are available within the nation; some may still be under abject poverty if availability is erratic with reference to place, time and to whom. A proper all inclusive distribution process is of utmost importance. Consequently monetary policy is of utmost importance to vanish poverty from a nation.

Acid tests of a good all inclusive Monetary Policy will be, as given in the following few pages:

1. Does it ensure that food is available to each and every citizen (including children, sick, weak, and/or not part of the work force)?

Food of any quality will not be sufficient for a strong nation; nourishing food to be made available to every individual; is government's responsibility.

This can be ensured only by (a) availability of food items aplenty (b) and at very low price to the final consumer and (c) low price of items is uniform for all citizens.

A nation where average monthly income is Rs. 2000/-, and most of the population is vegetarian, and is selling pulses (dals) and lentils at Rs. 50/- to Rs. 90/- per kg. definitely cannot ensure that all the citizens can buy dals for daily consumption (most of the population will not be able to afford) and the future of such a nation is doomed. If children do not get requisite proteins (dals are main sources) at the formative stage, that nation will have generations of citizens, in future, mentally and physically substandard, of low capability and huge health care bills. The same is true for vegetables, fruits and grains.

Proper distribution of food items to the citizens can only be ensured by prices of food items, which means nearly free. Targets may be Re. 1/- or Rs. 2/- per kg. for any and ever food item. Gradations on quality in a democracy is necessary and bound to happen, but a reasonably good quality must be available at Re. 1 to Rs. 2/- per kg. Good quality rice at Re. 1 or Rs. 2/- will ensure affordability by everybody. Same has to be for wheat, other grains, dals, vegetables and fruits and dairy items.

Basmati rice may be sold at Rs. 10/- kg or Rs. 20/- per kg; it is immaterial as long as kolam, jeerasai, ambemohar, adamchini, masuri are available at Re. 1/- per kg.

Some argue that wages or earnings of everybody should go up so that everyone can afford food. It is a fallacy and will never give the desired result. Best mechanism for equitable distribution is very low price of an item and the price remains applicable uniformly for all citizens.

As for a human, air is free, food also has to be nearly free, drinking water is to be nearly free and affordable to even the weakest of our society and our national brethrens.

How is it possible to do? It is possible to do this by ruthless, imaginative monetary policy of the governments. The white world of USA and most of the European nations have done this. Why not India?

Also, these nations, want the food items prices in India (and also in other poor or developing nations) to go up; because it serves their interest. The currency exchange rates will go in favour of their currency and exports from the developing nations will subsidize the rich living style of the citizens of those nations.

These developed nations will lecture the developing nations that there should be no agricultural subsidy, but the developed nations give the biggest agricultural subsidies to their farmers. These developed nations will say that the agri-subsidy is very less compared to the nations' GDP; but what should really be compared is the agri-subsidy per capita and then it will be found that 50-100 times of agri-subsidy of the developing nation like India is given by the developed nations.

Table 9: Agricultural Subsidy

Country	Annual Agricultural Subsidy		
	US$ billion	Approx. Rs. Crore	Approx. Per citizen Rs.
USA	58.899	273900	9040
European Union	121.265	563882	11480
Canada	6.769	31476	9480
Japan	56.858	264390	20800
India—		**34784**	**300**

India must increase direct and indirect agricultural subsidy substantially without any fear of internal or external bad impacts. This action is like pouring cement while making foundation for a strong building if nation is a building. Pour lot of quality cement i.e. pour lot of agricultural subsidy if the nation has to be strong and without poor people. Affordability of food with dignity is very important.

Besides agricultural subsidy for bringing the food prices down, it is important to reduce the manpower being used today for distribution. Milk is procured in Maharashtra state at

Annual Agriculture Subsidy/Citizen

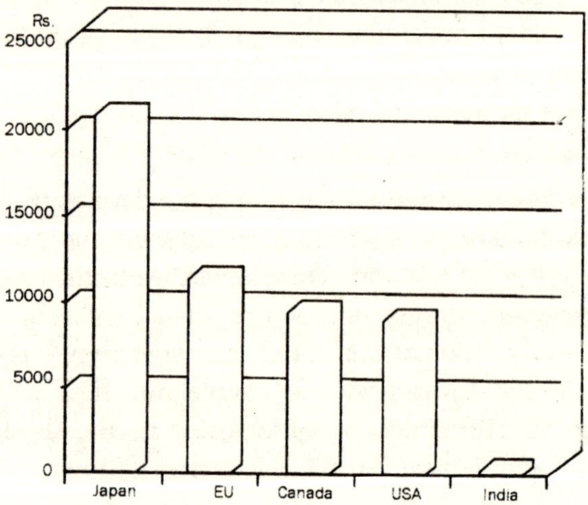

Rs. 12.50 per liter from the milk producer or farmer. But the same milk is sold after packaging at Rs. 25 per liter, roughly double. The packed milk selling companies work as middleman. Finally milk is sold to the citizen by the retailer. The milk packaging unit will say that they procure, transport and pasteurize the milk that makes it costlier. But in the process the milk has become so expensive that the poor households just do not have the money to buy the milk even for their children. There has to be a method to sell the milk at Rs. 15 per liter to the citizens, if procurement is happening at Rs. 12.50 per liter. The Rs. 12.50 procurement price is fixed by the government, but the final selling price is fixed by the packager. What logic is that? If government has the time and resources to fix the procurement price, at the same time, government can also fix the final price to the consumer. Middlemen/middle companies are making the whole economy expensive and the general public is the suffering lot. The milk example is true to all commodities and it is distorting the distribution pattern. A tiny percentage of population, these middlemen, persons employed by middle companies are creating havoc in the distribution pattern and creating poverty many fold times unbearable.

Actually, the whole system needs to have a paradigm shift. Aping of the western economic systems is making the life unbearable for most of the population of the developing world. If India has to succeed, it has to think differently. For the reasons of benefit to few individuals the majority is suffering the curse of poverty.

The persons released from this activity are not going to be unemployed. They will get used in actual creation of wealth. Every employment must be checked with the acid test: the person's contribution to creation of national wealth. The national wealth and personal wealth may or may not be same. Many times, quite often, if governance is poor, the personal wealth is not national wealth.

The low food items prices increase the intrinsic value and strength of the national currency.

2. Is land available for farming, cultivation/fruit production to a group of individuals (cooperative societies) nearly free but it is not free to the same individual at many places?

As for food production, is processing and retail space made available by government nearly free of cost?

- Area of India = 3287300000000 sq.m
- Population of India = 1147995000 (July, 2008)
- Area available per capita = 2863 sq.m
- If considering forests, rivers, lakes, utilities, only 2/3rd availability of land to individuals, area available per capita = 2863 x 0.66 = 1890 sq.m

Any group can be allotted his due of land i.e. 1890 sq.m multiplied by the number of people in the group for farming, cultivation or fruit cultivation or food processing. It will be simple justice with social benefit of encouraging food production.

Why this needs to be done? This needs to be done for the following reasons.

(a) Individuals having better resources tend to corner more land or space, for use in future, or speculation or no use.

(b) Humans like animals wish to mark territories; bigger the territory bigger food availability is an animal instinct and land hoarding becomes mentally satisfying.

To overcome this natural tendency; society, in turn government has to regulate. Also certain direction by monetary policy will ensure better productivity of the land.

If 10 people make an association and apply to government, the association to be allotted 1890 x 10 = 18900 sq. m of land nearly free of cost; if and only if, the use of the land is for food production. There has to be control and monitoring of the land use for the next 50 years at least.

Rich, industrialists, politicians and builders buy or get allocated land at throw away prices for speculation, or production of consumption goods not of basic needs. This is antinational activity. An organization getting allocated free land for itself and vendors to produce a small car is definitely antinational. If it is agricultural land it is criminal when so many mouths go hungry. Why those citizens of a country, who are not getting even one meal a day, should be giving their share of land (they also own the national land as much as those who can afford to keep a car.) Such free or subsidized allotment of land is subsidy in the wrong direction. Argument that employment generation will happen is illogical at the national level.

A nation which cannot feed all its citizens has no right to allot free or subsidized land for secondary industry. To allot subsidized or agricultural land for secondary industry and that too for subsidizing a small car price is a defective monetary policy. Small car project has been taken as example just because it brought awareness; but it is true for all luxury items or goods which do not fall in the category of satisfying basic, more fundamental human needs. At nation's level, employment generation is not an issue at all, but food production for everybody is a social, governmental and national primary task.

Industries, and even new townships, cities etc., should and must not be allowed to use away even an inch of fertile agricultural land; or land having potential for development as fruit plantation, or potential for any form of food production.

Even shifting of industries and townships from current locations, if on land, which could be used for agriculture to rocky, *banjar* land in the country is to be considered. In India there is no shortage of such land.

It is not that industries should not be encouraged; encouragement must be done since production of goods is creation of wealth. But in a country like India, food production must be given topmost priority and monetary policy to achieve food for all the citizens to be framed to guide this to happen in the shortest possible time.

3. Is the monetary policy making available reasonably good quality clothes for all its citizens?

After food availability this should be the second most important priority.

A torn clothing of an individual, makes that individual feel low in front of another who is wearing untorned clothes. No human being is inferior to another in a nation and it is not the individual's fault that he has no resources to cover himself properly. It is nation's responsibility to produce and provide cover to all of its citizens.

And if any citizen or some citizens are not able to afford clothing, it is national shame. If a sizeable section of the national population is not able to buy reasonably good quality clothing, it is bigger national shame.

When there was British rule over India and only a fraction of one percent of the Indian citizens could afford proper clothing, it was understandable since they never considered the Indian population as theirs and equal to themselves. But after independence, yes, a better percentage (over probably 20-30%) affords good clothings. But still sizeable percentage of the people is poor and cannot afford proper clothing. After independence the government has been of self rule, democratic government and why sizeable number of Indian citizens does not afford to get proper un-torned clothing? Are these governments (centre and states) treat their citizens same as British government?

Gradations of clothing material shape and designs are bound to happen in democracy. However a reasonably good quality of clothing material must be made available at nearly free price. This can be done very efficiently by the monetary policy. The costs of doing so is very small compared to the psychological boost for its citizens and boosts in individual image, national image, confidence levels of both individuals and nation.

- Target price for reasonable good quality clothing materials for gents and ladies = Rs. 3 to Rs. 5 per metre.
- Minimum 20 metres of clothing for a person is required per year.
- Total clothing material required per annum at the nation's level = P x 20 metres

  = 1150000000 x 20 metres

  = 23000000 000 metres
- Let us say, cost of production (including profit) is Rs. 35/- per metre.
- Total subsidy at national level if it is sold at Rs. 3/- per metre = Rs. 3223 000 000 000

  = Rs. 736 000 000 000

  = Rs. 73600 crores

For this small amount on the national level, think of the pride of all of its citizens covered in decent dress and not wearing torn clothes. What a national pride? 20 meters of clothing material every year for every person at Rs. 60/- only.

It does not mean it has to be one colour and one texture. It should be of various textures and colours and prints. It is feasible since the volume of production will be very high.

Only thing to be ensured will be that it does not get exported. If exported, then India will be clothing the whole world population instead of its own citizens. It would be just idiotic.

Availability of low price clothing will strengthen the currency too.

4. Is the monetary policy making available housing for all citizens?

Shelter is important to weather the heat, cold and rain. Do children have place to study and play?

(a) New well planned townships to be developed on lands which are unproductive, non-agricultural, have no food production potential. We have enough of only rock lands in every state. This makes the lands free on national basis thereby reducing the price of the housings and townships.

(b) Such lands may be given to builders and developers free or almost free with a condition of certain amenities to be provided in the housing complex or the townships.

(c) Governments should ensure that long lasting (50 to 100 years), low cost (i.e. uses less of natural resources for the building materials) and reasonable accommodations (not bird's nest size) are built in big numbers and sold at very low prices.

Building such houses/accommodations does not need money at the national level as explained earlier. It is just a question of determination, planning, monetary policy and ruthless implementation.

The above does not mean that luxurious houses/ accommodations will not be built and sold. In a democracy this will happen and let it be so as a free enterprise.

But well built accommodations for all citizens to be built and provided by the monetary policy of the governments.

Building materials for such houses/accommodations is to be produced on mass scale. This again does not need money at the nation's level. It is just determination, planning, monetary policy and ruthless implementation.

5. Is the monetary policy providing meaningful education to all the citizens—young, youth, old, boys, girls, men and women?

At present the answer to the above is "NO".

According to the international literacy norm (and it seems reasonable), i.e. read, write, do basic mathematical sums and class V pass, India has over 600 million (600000 000 persons) illiterate citizens. It means approximately 50% of Indian population is illiterate. Only 6.5% of population study beyond 12th Standard.

We have to move fast on the educational front if poverty has to be vanished.

(a) 29 million (29000000) babies are born every year in India. The nation must have primary school for these children. If every school admits on an average 20 children every year at the entry level, number of schools required = 29000000/20 = 1450000 i.e. fourteen and half lakh primary schools.

India has 970 000 schools. Minimum requirement of number of primary schools is 15 lakhs. India must target to double the number of primary schools on crash basis considering remote areas where even 10 students may not be able to reach to a school, what to talk of 20 average. Aim to be that every child has right to a school even if the school is for one child. Most of these schools need to be opened in the villages especially remote areas. China has 1800000 (18 lakhs) schools already and yet continuing to build.

It is not big money to build many lakh of primary schools on the national level but future benefit will be immense. The whole thing can be implemented in a year if properly planned. The decision for locations probably will take more time (3 to 4 months if seriously taken), implementation could be quickly done.

(b) Locations of primary schools should be such that no tender age child has to come for more than 2 km from his home to attend school.

(c) The school dropout rate in India is very high, 90–94%. The educationists and researchers on the subject have/will come out with many reasons and all are definitely valid. The ways and means to overcome/eliminate each of these reasons are to be implemented expeditiously.

But "LURE THE CHILD" concept will give instant benefit in reducing the drop-out rate to below 10%. Child will force the parents to accept the child being in the school.

To lure the child to school:

1. Play garden with play accessories in every primary school. Providing these does not cost anything.
2. Structured plenty of time in play accompanied with simple learning.
3. Every child loves fruits and most love Milk. Periodic serving of these two items especially fruits (safe and easy serving) will bring the child back to school next day.
4. Good clothing to be provided to every child so as not to have comparative inferiority complex.
5. No demands on parents. Every child up to class V is the state's responsibility. He is not an extra mouth to be fed; he is a national resource and must be cultivated for future of the nation.

(d) Standard VI (6) to standard XII (12): most of the young population must go through.

Standard VI to VIII: Location of school for the child not to commute more than 4 kms.

Standard IX to XII: Location of school/college for the boy/girl not to commute more than 6 kms.

University/professional/Vocational Education: Location of the institution for the girls/boys/young woman/young man not to commute more than 10 kms.

The above will require:

Table 10: Schools/Colleges/Universities/Professional Colleges or Institutes

(a) India New Requirement

	Primary	Std. VI-VIII	Std. X-XIII	University/ Institutes	Vocational Training Centres
Current availability	970000	@	18000	360	1000
Total requirement	1500000	330000	153000	10000	100000
New to be built	530000	530000	135000	9640	99000
Assume budget per school for building	30 lac	50 lac	1 crore	20 crore	3 crore
Total fund reqmt.	159000 crore	165000 crore	135000 crore	193000 crore	297000 crore

The total fund requirement for all the buildings of the above new requirements of schools, colleges, universities, institutes and vocational training centers works out to 949000 crore to be spent in 5 years which works out to just 18.6%

@ The number is included in primary and colleges.

of India's central government's 2009-10 expenditure estimate. If state governments also pitch in, all that new educational buildings requirement comes out from government, owned by governments and the management for running may be government cum private. It is feasible to create all the above educational schools and colleges and institutes and the vocational centers. The benefit of the same will be for at least 100 years.

It is sad that Central Government subsidies in the year 2008-09 on petrol, diesel, kerosene and cooking gas amounted to Rs. 103000 crore which mainly serves a particular section of the population. If these fuel subsidies were transferred to education sector, along with other allocations to education sector every year, the total combined resource will pay for quality education of all Indians up to a level which will make the economic growth of the nation fly in the sky.

The above projections for total and new requirements are not out of proportion. China created 1 170000 (over 11 lac) schools two decades ago and their economy has been growing the fastest.

First priority is to be for primary schools, the resource requirement per primary school is also the lowest but number of schools required is also huge. Next to be the middle school and then higher secondary (intermediate) colleges and Vocational Technical Training Centers. Though resource requirement is the highest for university, engineering and medical colleges, these are also important. The chart for resource requirement per unit as given below clarifies the same.

Though the resource requirements for each levels of education are different, we lag in quantity and quality both at all levels. Hence it is desired that over a period of 5 years, total resources in each segment or levels of education are to be of the same order. The new units required also more or less depict the same except for the vocational technical training

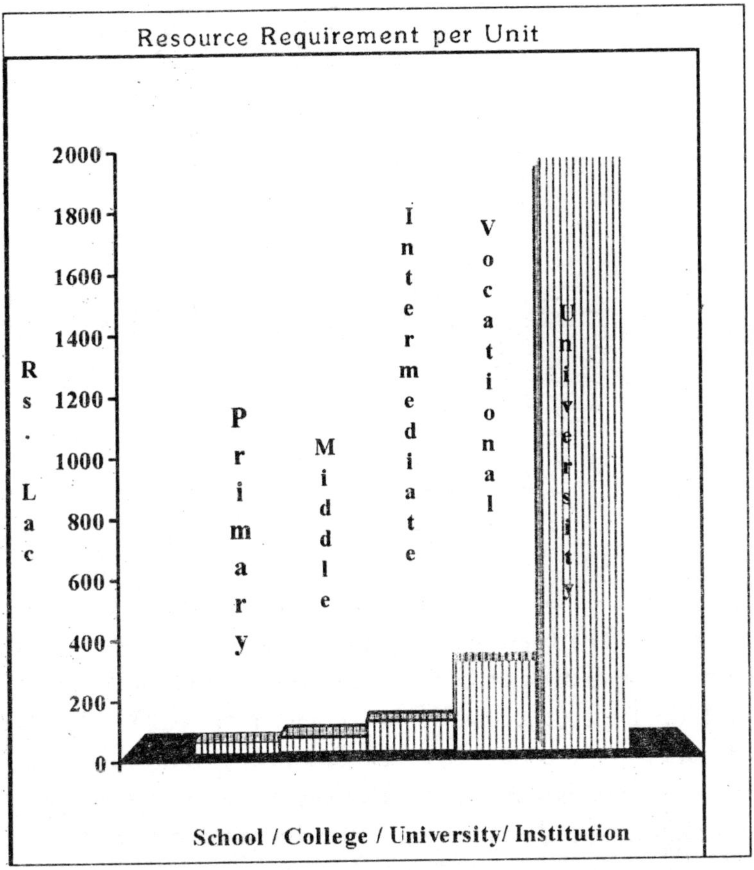

centers. For vocational technical training centers the requirement for opening additional centers is shown approximately double. This is necessary considering that at very nominal resource deployment the employability of the citizens can be appreciably enhanced, also quick increase will follow in quality and quantity for creation of national wealth. The chart below depicts visually the proportions of resource requirements in different levels (segments) of education at the national level for creating new facilities.

India allocated for the first time 5.30% of GDP on education for year 2009-10. Earlier years the percentage used

Resource requirment over 5 years for various educational streams

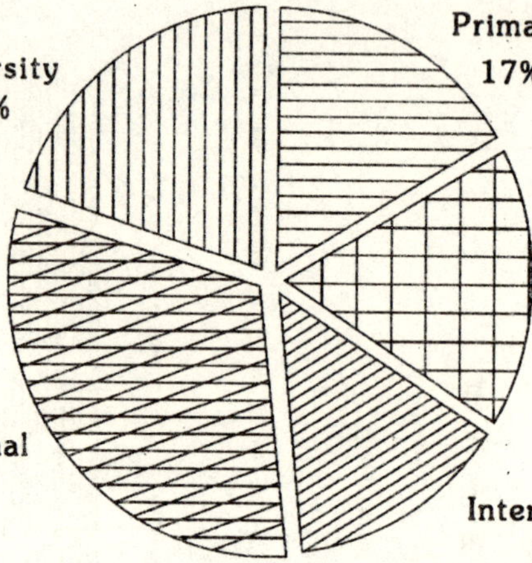

to be much lower. It must go up to 15% to 20% of GDP on education. There are many countries which allocate much higher than 5.30% of GDP on education. And India has to catch up. If India allocates 15 to 20 percent of its GDP towards education for the next 5 to 10 years only, the profile and complexion of citizens and the nation will change dramatically. Afterwards, the allocation may even be reduced to half.

Table 11: Educational Expenditure

Country	*Approx annual education budget Rs. crore*	*Approx annual education budget allocation per citizen Rs.*
USA	3530500	115000
UK	579500	95000
India	**38000**	**320**

Presenting the above data for visual comparison in a chart form:

Educational Expenditure

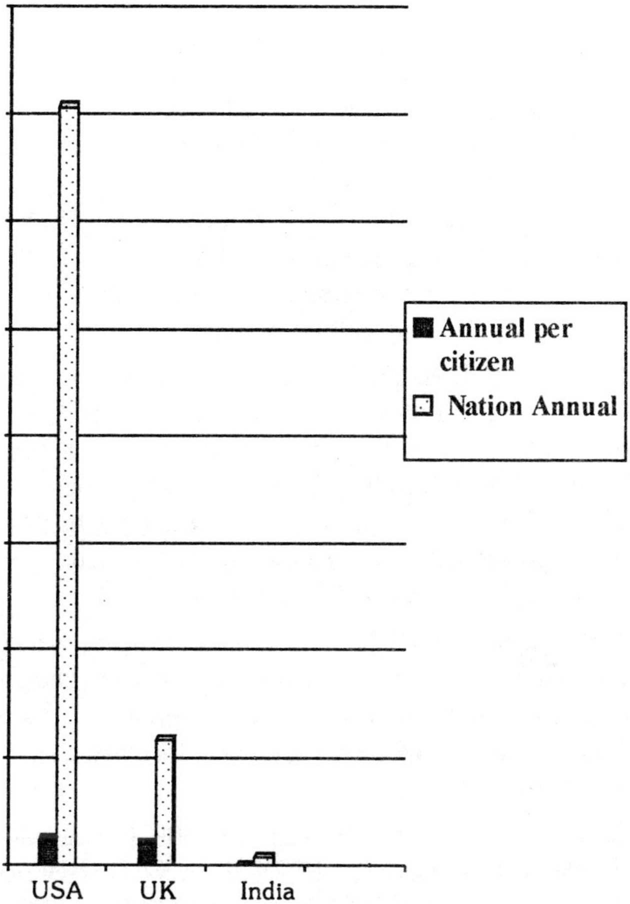

Actually the budget allocation for education is to be 10 to 15% of the total revenue of centre and state governments, showing clear cut priority of the governments.

There should be emphasis on science subjects, professional training, industrial training and vocational training, there must be emphasis on developing mental faculty of analysis, reasoning and synthesis for every child, young man. These are the foundations on which National House should be built, so as the same lasts longer.

Global polity, and also our polity have spoiled the cultural and social fabric of hard work, honesty, truthfulness and justice. These are the traits in a human being to be valued. Today opposite of these are being valued leading to human unhappiness. Today a group of individuals create castles based on smartness, dishonesty, lies and injustice. This leads to unhappiness of many who are impacted by such an organization. Sometimes, though rarely, those who build these castles also ultimately get unhappiness. Such castles are very common in industries and politics nowadays.

But a national development programme needs individuals who have personality traits of hard work, honesty, truthfulness and justice. These are to be cultivated as inborn qualities. It becomes easier to cultivate these traits (i) if emphasized from very childhood (ii) parents practice the same (iii) when basic needs of an individual/family are met (iv) when society looks down on those who practice the opposites.

Spirituality and not religion is to be encouraged. Why not develop Indian Spiritual Essence which every Indian voluntarily follows irrespective of cast, creed, religion or region. This will add to the citizens' happiness and will increase National Happiness Index.

India's national budget estimates for 2009-10 was having total expenditure estimate of Rs. 1020838 crore. This consisted of Non-Plan expenditure of 695689 crore and Plan expenditure of 325149 crore.

On education the budget was having Plan expenditure of mere Rs. 36175 crore i.e. 3.54% of total expenditure or 11.13% of Plan expenditure.

There is declining priority of education in the public policy paradigm in India. This needs to be reversed by appreciable enhancement of target allocation for education; it should have been at least 15% of the total expenditure of annual budget i.e. Rs. 153130 crore.

This big enhancement on education should be done in one stroke while making next budget allocation coupled with an announcement that this will be the percentage of allocation towards education for at least 10 years in future. This action will give maximum ROCI (return on capital investment) for a nation, especially for India. And the money is to be directed for building world class (really better than world class) campuses consisting of University or Institute buildings, excellent quality totally green buildings for Primary Schools, Secondary Schools, Colleges, Vocational Technical Training Centers for the first 3 years and then later enhancing infrastructure of teachers, libraries, instruments, etc.

Summary

- *Monetary policy is very important in removing poverty i.e. in production of wealth and its distribution to citizens.*
- *Essential and basic food items have to be nearly free to all citizens. It is feasible to do so by conscious selected government decisions of subsidizing inputs in agriculture and supplementary food items production, direct from production point to final customer.*
- *At present maximum employment is in agriculture and food items production, processing and distribution. By mechanization, there have to be least employment in agriculture and food items production, processing and distribution.*

  Employment in this sector to be reduced to 1/3 of what is today.

- *Land and real state speculation to be stopped. Real estate as an investment option to be closed. Bring down input costs in building of accommodations. Decent shelters to all citizens is a must.*
- *At least one or two types of cloth material to be available to all citizens nearly free or at nominal costs.*
- *Subsidy and assistance on all other sectors of economy to be withdrawn except food, clothing and house building industries and its input materials industries at least for 10 years.*
- *Education is to be made as very important focus for the next 10 years.*

To remove poverty in 5 years, public policies to be defined for long term, a minimum for 10 years, to commit to the directions and seriousness today. It will also show the general public that government will make policies only what is beneficial to most of the citizens and not for certain selected classes.

In a country like India, every Central Government policy to be checked for its utility for at least to 1/10th of population, i. e., benefit to 12 crore (minimum number) citizens. Similarly the acid check is to be for State Governments, a policy or decision must benefit at least 1/10th population of the state.

Chapter - 12

NECESSITY OF STANDARDIZATION

Creation of uniformity in any commodity, item, process, and thinking is standardization. Sometimes forced uniformity robs the freedom, robs the innovative spirit, and even may rob democratic values. But for those who are hungry, who are naked, who have only sky as roof; these words freedom, innovative spirit, democracy are meaningless, hollow and crooked. They think these have been created for cheating them by those who have somehow all of it though they were created equal.

To avoid wastage of resources (manpower, time, national wealth), it is imperative to create, adapt and use standardization as a process in all walks of life. Creation of standards is to be responsibility of central government and a full fledged ministry (equivalent to Home Ministry) will not be impertinent. The Central Government must pass a law granting authority for the development of central catalogue and standardization programme.

Benefits of Standardization

If there is necessity to build and open 100000 primary schools all over the country—there are many ways to do the same.

Process A: Every state government is told to do so. Then each state government tells the districts to do the same. And then these district authorities start looking at the land requirement, get the design of the building from consultants, look for implementation of the order in all aspects.

Process B: Another approach could be to appoint an agency to create a standard for primary school, for all aspects of a primary school creation and maintenance. Catalogue is created for all the items required in creation of a primary school. These standards are made available to all the state governments and all district administrations. The plan is communicated to the state governments. The implementation procedure is followed as per the standards.

A table below with some indicative figures is created just to drive home the benefits of standardization.

For school creation

	Process A	*Process B*	*Remarks*
Manpower in terms of man-hours	240000	60000	Process B needs 1/4th manpower resource
Time (months)	12	4	Process B needs 1/3rd time resource
Quality of work	Maybe good or maybe bad	Will be good	Quality gets improved and assured
Wastage of materials	Sure to be high	Controlled	

The example shows enormous savings of resource requirements and guarantee of quality of work to a great extent. The saving in time for implementation is humungous.

If there are 100000 primary schools to be opened, the impact for the whole nation by opting for standardization will be great in terms of savings in time, resources of manpower and material. The schools will be of uniform quality all over the country and will not be dependent on the whims and idiosyncrasies of the administrators and local bodies. The manpower which will not be required for creating the primary schools will get used in creation of other national wealth.

Primary schools example has been taken just to show the benefits. Truly, if numbers of anything to be produced is more, standardization will deliver big economic benefits. It should be used for creation of all national wealth: roads, bridges, canals, joining of rivers, creation of schools, colleges, universities, professional colleges, railway lines, bogies, ships, satellites, aero planes, fighters. To generate national wealth in fastest manner, lean on standardization of most of the aspects– physical, safety, technology, procedural, accounting, etc.

Standardization is one of the guru-mantras for quick removal of poverty—made possible even in five years.

Laundry list of Advantages of Standardization

1. Colossal reduction in resource requirements in design, development, installation, training, startup, and maintenance.
2. Minimizes glitches in quality. Eliminates need for testing and evaluation for subsequent implementations.
3. Enormous saving in time.
4. Increasing safety.
5. Improving design with less special efforts.
6. **Improves communication:** Standards create a common language on parts identification, service requirements, processes, safety, etc. during implementation and maintenance.
7. In some cases, reduces need to maintain high inventories of spares, parts, etc. and improves availability due to scale of operations, interchangeability of parts and components.

8. Insures use of latest technology and quick changes for improvement due to technological innovations. Also, quicker development of new or improved technology is facilitated by standardization process. In nutshell:
   (a) quicker deployment of new technology and
   (b) faster development of new technology.
9. Provides practical application of experts' knowledge, representing years of experience and avoids necessity of starting each project from ground up.
10. Standardization in Technology.
11. Simplified support and training—use of standards and standard platforms simply demand less training and specialization during subsequent implementation.
12. Allows use of less specialized or unskilled manpower without sacrificing quality during subsequent application rollouts.
13. Encourages item standardization.
14. Improves specifications.
15. Creation of a critical mass for decision making.
16. Bringing economy of scale in procurement with added improvement in negotiating power on quality and technology. This benefit makes buying decisions faster and simpler to make.
17. Standardization is one of the key processes of knowledge management. It is an excellent tool in collection, structuring, storing and using of knowledge. At national level for a big country like India knowledge management is one of the fundamental pillars to support all inclusive sustained development.
18. **Saves administrative entanglement:** comments, accusations, blames, litigation reduce drastically if good standardization has been created and implemented.
19. **Reduces corruption potential:** standardization definitely robs away many opportunities for corruption at different stages of implementation.

Risks of Standardization

At times there are disadvantages too of going for standardization or rather risks of (bad) standardization:

(a) Risk of preventing innovation or slowing down or postponing innovation. Innovation is at its peak when many flowers are permitted to bloom.

(b) Risk of not creating variety though the same may be desired. Though within the variety, there may be high standardization. To understand it better, that if dance forms would have been standardized all over the country in olden days, then we would not have had so many dance varieties like Bharatnatyam, Odissi, Kathak, Bihu, Manipuri, Odissi, etc. But within each dance form, there is sophisticated standardization. It may be necessary to have variety of passenger planes having different seating capacity but the same may get overlooked for standardization sake in a nation.

(c) Agencies which create standards may tend to incorporate unnecessary complexity.

(d) It is used by many countries to create barriers for imports. It may be a blessing in disguise for developing world. Or, it may lead to ignorantly avoiding some new developments elsewhere.

Any action has both sides of coin and there has to be a balance and open eyes to get maximum benefit. The benefits flowing due to standardization process remarkably and definitely outweigh some risks of the standardization process. As mentioned earlier, actually the risks are results of bad standardization process. Hence, the same have a tendency to get mitigated or minimized if the process is made robust enough. It is made robust by training, researching of local conditions, keeping fresh outlook and always looking for opportunity to improve processes.

Barriers and Challenges in Standardization

There are certain barriers faced when trying to put standardization in place. These are mainly due to different perceptions in performance, or interoperability (various departments and agencies), availability of a resource or difference in opinion regarding criticality of an issue or item in the process. There has to remain sustained focus to remove any barriers encountered for standardization considering the prime goal of economic benefits of standardization

Challenges faced in standardization emanate mainly from the demand on quality and demand on features. The standardization organization's responsibility includes incorporating clauses and processes ensuring the best quality and whereas the vendors and manufacturers always put pressure to dilute the quality or to lower the requirements. Similarly, pressure may be put by manufacturers or service providers to include specific features which are only offered by them.

Relevant businesses or manufacturing organizations should be roped in early while formulating standards, since businesses not only reduce the economic risk of their R&D activities by participating in standardization, but tend to lower their R&D costs too. When a company influences the content of standards to its advantage, the economic risk gets mitigated. Studies have reinforced general belief that R&D costs are lower since the company comes to know the requirements in advance and also by cooperating on R&D efforts with others in the same or similar business. Standardization reduces to a great extent duplication of R&D efforts since results of previous studies normally are available.

How do standardization processes work?

Standardization processes are carried out in many different types of organizations on a national, regional and global level. Mostly, standardization is conducted following a number of identical process steps.

These process steps are:

- Need Identification.
- Formulation of objectives and requirements. These could be functional, user or commercial.

- Drafting of specifications and the standard by a group of technical experts of the specific area and also of the related areas.
- Formal approval process: It may be within the organization or may be referred to a wider audience. Normally a wider audience is invited when it is felt that support of others is necessary for smooth implementaion of the standard or it will help in further standardization process.
- Implementaion process is initiated. This may include testing of the standard, coordination aspects within various implementation agencies, impact of local conditions, etc.
- Periodic Review to update the standard to keep the standard in harmony with time, technology and experience.

In order to interface with standard bodies in efficient way, any project must take above steps into account while determining work packages, while allocating resources, and while planning deliverables. Despite these general process characteristics there will also be differences between processes.

Which type of standardization process should a project pursue?

There are formal and non-formal standardization organizations. There are legal or mandatory standards or only as guidelines.

What type of standard and organization for the same is required is dependent on the objectives.

If 100000 primary schools need to be opened having best quality and educational standards in the shortest span of time, it will be necessary to go for formal organization for making the standards and the output of the organization will be both mandatory standards and guideline standards. The size, the buiding design construction and its architecture, schools facilities, etc. will need to be of mandatory nature to achieve resource, time and quality requirements. The teaching and course structures may be of guidelines type of standards to allow local aspirations of language, skills, etc.

To take another example, if there are so many bus stops to be made all over the country, standards must be created for the structure, for the protection, for may be vegetable and fruit stalls adjoining the bus stops to bring thoughtful facilities, long life, aesthatic looks and also for revenue by advertisement.

Choosing a formal standards body is the best route if ultimate objective is to have the standards made mandatory or legal to follow.

Non-formal standardization organization is created to gain, impart knowledge and supports, and most of the time is prelude to more formal organization.

What should be standardized?

Most aspects of each and every development project will get expedited and huge economic benefits will accrue if standardization is made part of the process of project initiation and implementation.

Necessity of standardization can best be understood and appreciated if nature is taken as example. In nature, wherever, whatever, whenever is looked upon, is an example of standardization. Nature, has great and immaculate standardization process though there is so much of diversity.For example, all higher level mammals have two eyes, one nose, two ears, one mouth, five fingers, etc. Rather all body parts have been standardised in function and construction though allowing variability of size, shape, looks, etc. within specific ranges. An adult human height is variable but within a range, there is no human who will have five metres height. Heart may vary somewhat in size and shape but the function will remain of pumping for blood circulation.

Great care has been taken by nature for standardization to reduce chaos and for smooth functioning of the creation with all its glitches, diversity and vastness. Consequences of all humans not having standardizsed focal length of eyes (each person having different focal length of lens in eyes) are unimaginable. Even spectacles would have not got invented. Most of the nature's processes in the universe are standardized and that is how the generation of term 'universal process' happened. A big nation's processes are vast and standardization is necessary for reduction of chaos and for smooth functioning.

India is not new to standardization. It had created Indian Standards Institute way back in history. In 1987, Bureau of Indian Standards (BIS) replaced the Indian Standards Institute. Bureau if Indian standards is a national standards body under the Ministry of Consumer Affairs, Food and Public Distribution, Government of India. It has regional offices in metros and branch offices in various cities. It also does some certification work for various industries. But overall its scope and actual work is very very limited.

For faster national development, for 100% removal of poverty, for total removal of poverty in five years; standardisation is absolute requirement at the national level. Hence the suggestion is hereby made of creating a central government 'Ministry of Standardization and Catalogues' having home ministry stature and importance. The benefit of this move for national development will be collosal and all pervading. The benefit towards development becoming all inclusive will be categorically visible.

Summary

- *Standardisation has too many benefits to be ignored.*
- *It must be given national importance to get the immense economic benefits to the nation.*

- *It greatly reduces resource requirement and the implementation time frame.*
- *To remove poverty and progress of the nation at the break neck speed, all facets of governance and projects to make standardization as essential feature.*
- *Periodic review of standards is necessary to avoid disadvantages/risks of standardization.*

The Government to legislate formation of "Ministry of Standardization and Catalogues" at the earliest.

Chapter - 13

IMPACT OF CORRUPTION

That monarch, whose subjects are carried from his kingdom by ruffians, while they call aloud for protection and he barely looks on them with his ministers, is a dead, and not a living king.

—*Manusmriti* VII/143

There is no nation free of corruption; there is no government free of corruption. It inheres in all social systems and government systems. It has been and will be present in each and every monarchy, democracy, socialism, communism, capitalism, feudalism, caste system, religious system, various classes of society, every gender and in all age groups and in all times. It is all pervading human society's evil and has wide ranging losses to every human society. It cannot be eliminated, but it can be reduced effectively and every one must aid in reducing corruption to minimize the impact.

Is *Manusmriti* valid today and that too in democracy? It is. A recent example of events proves the happening in a democracy. Take the case of one of the states in India. All residents of a state, if they are Indian nationals, are the subjects of the state government and the central government. Some subjects (migrated from other states) were being harassed by some, and governments were looking aside. Is it not a form of political corruption? *Manusmriti* is emphasizing nothing but political corruption and its outcome or result.

There are many forms and manifestations of corruption and it will not be dealt in detail here since that will not serve the objectives of this book. However, corruption has many severe impacts on some sub-processes, time frame and final deliverables in the overall development process of a nation. Public policy has definitely to be tailored to minimize the impacts of corruption.

There are a few who even argue that corruption is beneficial for a developing nation and bribe brings efficiency to the process by expediting the outcome, but these are the vested interests whose personal interests are served by perpetuating the corruption in the socio-economic systems. It is better to ignore them and silence them by aggressively refuting the same. Their logic is biased since some other person is definitely going to be a victim, who does not pay the bribe, of delays or unfavourable, unjustified decision making process.

Though there are so many types and forms of corruption, the development process is most affected by political corruption and the impact throwing a development project towards its death may be very severe. Enron power project example in the recent history is known to all. A nation's development may suffer to such great extent that it may take years, decades or some time even centuries to recover. Many generations of citizens suffer by being hungry, ill-clothed and roofless. History is full of such examples. Indian citizens suffered and lived miserable lives under foreign rule, foreign rule made possible due to foreign and indigenous political corruptions. Recent example is the food price rise during 2009/2010, doubling and tripling the food prices, thereby throwing a vast population back to degradable poverty, the population which had just overcome the poverty line in the last 20 years. It has thrown the nation back by at least 20 years. The sudden price rise is not due to sudden shortages in production, it is not due to sudden population explosion, it is not due to hoarding by unsocial elements, it is not by middle men; its main cause is the political corruption—subsidy on exports, exports even when there are domestic shortages, imports at higher prices, sometimes probably import of the same what was exported earlier, all this by certain vested interests. In the name of farmers benefit, food prices to be higher, but average farmers do not really get benefited, ultimately they also will have to pay higher for everything, and ultimately they are hungry, coverless and roofless.

Political corruption results in the following:

1. Systemic corruption in the administration—bureaucracy, approvals and sanctions, judiciary, all wings of governance.
2. Systemic corruption in businesses and business environment
3. Systemic corruption in social advocacy and influence groups.
4. Gives rise to business politicians or gain politicians who are interested only in self benefits.
5. Gives rise to bad laws and legislations serving only the nexus.
6. Gives rise to gangs and criminality.
7. Gives rise to class differentiation and exploitation.
8. Gives rise to chaotic, regional, local, political groups which sap the administration, which otherwise should concentrate on development issues.
9. Shortages of resources during execution of development projects.
10. No initiation and resource allocation for basic requirements since corruption thrives in environment of illiteracy, poverty and lawlessness.
11. Delays in execution of development projects.

12. Marked regional differences in development.
13. Welfare allocations never reach the targets, due to diversion, theft, loot and robbery by others.
14. Sometimes leads to death of a development project, often urgently needed one.
15. Leads to moral degradation and distorted value system in a community or society.
16. Sometimes leads to killing of a nation's own citizens even innocent ones.

Remedial actions are not easy to put in place because generally corrupts are in the power to frame the rules and sympathetic class consciousness of the politicians. All politicians consider themselves as of ruling class irrespective of attainment of power positions or otherwise. So mitigation of political corruption requires sustained efforts on the part of citizens and also of honest advocacy groups. Effects of various measures are limited in scope and degree. There is no one remedy of this disease.

However, all remedial actions have to target significant opportunity structures for influence peddling, and enhancement of morality and probity in public life.

Also one must keep in view that all politicians or all industrialists are not corrupt. Some are definitely honest but general perception about these professions of society is otherwise.

Right to Information Act (2005) is a laudable legislation in this direction in India. Some other pieces of legislation are also necessary to avoid both real and perceived political corruption.

Politics is not to be made a career

(a) No elected member for more than 2 terms in lifetime.

(b) No benefits or perks for lifetime to any legislator.

(c) High salary for the period of service. Salary linked to qualification.

(d) No position of office (minister, member of committee, member of board) etc. unless the individual is qualified having basic degree of graduation.

Nexus of politics, business and crime to be broken

(a) Governments to do governance only in select areas and rest to democracy. Present focus could be only on poverty removal, education, defence, science and technology and arts and culture.

(b) Public policies only if beneficial to a large population. Example: Whether stock market goes up or down is to be ignored by government since trading on stock market does not create national wealth. Criterion of creation of national wealth and equitable distribution may be a good test question for any public policy till it is assured and confirmed that all citizens get food, clothing and roof above.

(c) Penalties on politicians for not following any rule which is meant for consumption of general public too to be much more severe than any other citizen. For example not having a PAN Card, not filing or filing incorrectly the election expenditure, to have punishment of very high order.

(d) It is mandatory for Industrial Organizations to publish widely their income and expenditures on quarterly basis. Similarly it should be mandatory for all political parties to publish their income and expenditure every quarter widely.

(e) Police reforms to be taken up immediately.

Public opinion on morality, good values, and antipathy to corruption to be inculcated and strengthened by education in schools, by media, etc.

As mentioned earlier, a nation may ignore corruption for some time to come if it does not interfere in the execution of creation of national wealth. Politicians know and can effectively control this aspect if they wish to. Rather, if more national wealth gets created, their share of booty also goes up. Politicians must initiate, project, canvass, and fight for more, bigger, larger development projects benefiting vast sections of population. This will be to their benefit today and also for votes next time. They should desist in lobbying and influencing for such projects which benefit only limited number of people or certain class of people. In long term this is detrimental to their interests as aptly emphasized by *Manusmriti*.

Corruption does and will affect the distribution aspects in the elimination of poverty. Some will get more benefit than others. It may be ignored for expediency if sizeable general benefits accrue to most of the citizens. After all beyond a point, money in the bank or huge property becomes meaningless for any individual and remains idle. As for as nation is concerned; it will have to just print some extra currency notes not in use. It may safely be ignored.

Summary

- *Political corruption needs to be reduced.*
- *There are steps available to do so.*
- *It is beneficial to politicians to initiate and bat for big ticket development projects generating national wealth.*

Focus is not corruption during break-neck development; corruption is connected with money which is not necessary for creation of national wealth. But corruption does affect the distribution of wealth, distribution gets biased. The same may be ignored to some extent if larger benefits accrue to large sections of population. However, in the long range political corruption must be kept in check and at low level to create societal moral and value systems conducive to social harmony and peaceful living.

Chapter - 14

Developmental Mindsets and Attitudes

I used to think I was poor. Then they told me I wasn't poor, I was needy. They told me it was self defeating to think of myself as needy, I was deprived. Then they told me underprivileged was overused, I was disadvantaged. I still don't have a dime. But I have a great vocabulary.

—Jules Feiffer

Let all citizens be wealthy, let all work towards this end.

In development of a nation, nothing matters more than mindsets and attitudes of those who are involved in the process, especially in the leadership positions and planning process.

The nations which have removed poverty and moved on to become strong economies, had to initially and quickly focus on the change of mindsets and attitudes of its citizens and of the government administration. Deng Xiaoping's {a leader in the Communist Party of China (CPP)} famous saying 'Some must get rich first' in a communist setup echoes the role of change of mindset. For removal of poverty in a short period, it may be said '*Let all citizens be wealthy*'.

'Let all citizens be wealthy' statement also echoes 'all inclusiveness' besides its direction of change of attitude towards wealth—especially national wealth which is owned, shared, and created by the citizens, for the citizens.

What mindset will lead to 'let all citizens be wealthy'? It is the mindset of being "*Udyogi*". *A person who is Udyogi – fosters and values Innovation, Creativity, Hard Work and Creation of Wealth.* This mindset of being *Udyogi* will be one of the key tools of the process of total removal of poverty; if all citizens are with *Udyogi* mindset the nation will achieve social cohesion and reduce social exclusion.

Udyogi mindset refers to a citizen's ability to turn ideas into actions. This will need application of mind in creativity, innovation, risk taking, planning and management of projects in time and quality.

For removal of poverty, it will be necessary to change the existing mindset of thinking derived out of colonial mentality and thinking derived out of shortages. *The planners, the government, the private sector, the public sector all have to be dreamers of big things, superlative adjectives– whatever is to be done, whatever is to be built, whatever is created or produced from now on– it will be the best in the world, it will be the biggest in the world, most technologically advanced in the world, of longest life of the item in the world.* The aim has to be that whatever will be built, created, produced will be beyond match, better than in any other nation. This way of thinking, is absolutely necessary to get on the activities described in this book. This mindset raises the confidence level of the nation and also of each citizen. This mindset gets done more in shorter period. This mindset will create unmatched, never achieved earlier national wealth in the shortest period. When national pride goes up, big things happen on its own. Also this mindset will foster homogenous cohesive, result oriented team work. Big things can be achieved in modern times by teamwork– team members thinking big and implementing big, and of course getting trained to make best and big dreams to fruition.

Social values matter a lot, if a society and culture has to be built which lasts for ever; the values of *hard work, honesty, empathy, and pride are the four basic pillars of foundation.*

Attitude of positive thinking is essential for anything to get done. Attitude of negative thinking is suicidal since it only puts impediments in the process of anything good happening.

Following are few anecdotes/observations in real life. When you read and visualize the situation, do you see anything wrong? If yes, what is your view?

(a) At Kolkata airport, I arrive from Pune at 9.00 am. I have to catch a train at 5.30 pm and nothing to do in between. Somehow I am at airport manager's office and see a board that there are retiring rooms/dormitory facilities to accommodate over 70 people.

However, the booking clerk is not ready to allot and reason given is that I should have an air ticket showing journey to be made within 24 hours. Then I meet the airport manager, he cites the same rule. It is pointed out to him that the facility is for the ease and comfort of the passengers, it should be available to both outgoing and incoming passengers and there is not a single passenger in the dormitory having 15 beds. After persuasion and logic, he does see the reason and authorizes allotment

(b) On the 4th floor of a big building are the retiring rooms, a very good facility for large number of passengers, but the whole place has only a few occupants. On the second floor of the building, there is a restaurant. No takers and very bad quality of food and service.

(c) While waiting at the railway station, there are no benches on the platform and when inquired it was told that earlier wooden benches were there but were stolen. That was few years before.

(d) At one of the stations in M.P., at 8.45 in the night, 3 tier passengers finish their dinner and train has halted. The railway bearer has collected the *thalis* (dish plates) and stacked those at the platform. A young boy of 8-10 years age starts eating the left-over in the *thalis*. The railway catering bearer notices this, starts beating the boy and lifts him and bumps the boy against the sidewall of the staircase.

(e) At one of the railway stations in Karnataka, the train I was travelling had a stop and the site was of a well developed young man of 25 years age eating out of *thalis* collected and kept on the platform. Two goats are also eating from the same plate. Man seemed to be highly scared of the arrival of catering bearer at the station, his eyes rolling suspiciously around.

(f) At Mumbai we go for lunch at a medium size restaurant and the boy cleaning the table is hardly 14 years of age.

(g) I go to my village and by chance I happen to meet my 5th standard classmate. When asked what you do for living; his answer is that he collects iron items here and there on the nearby road. What about food? He looks around to save his face and replies– he is dependent on others, courtesies.

(h) Now-a-days even in the ordinary restaurants, after food, hot water and a piece of lemon is served to clean wash the hands.

(i) In big cities, it is difficult to walk or drive on main roads due to pollution.

All of us come across similar happenings in day-to-day life in India. Views differ and hence I give my views and leave space on the side for recording of your own views if you differ.

My View	Your View
(a) Lack of conceptual training (innovation)	
(b) Consequential of 1	
(c) Lack of detail planning and also lost sensitivity of railway authorities. (negative attitude)	

(d) Poverty of the boy and also of the railway canteen bearer.

(e) Naked poverty visible every where and hence sensitivity of the general public is dulled.

(f) Poverty affecting the future generation, future of nation.

(g) National planning gone haywire.

(h) Nothing wrong if national prosperity allows for the most citizens.

Presently in India where most are undernourished, this needs research for alternate and making the alternate popular.

(i) National Planning gone haywire {especially when examples were/are known outside the country}.

These 9 examples bring out that–

1. Abundance of poverty in India {all know}.
2. General sensitivity to ugly sights related to poverty is lost {all know}.
3. As a nation, we are unable to plan/implement even for simple things like vehicles density on urban roads {all know}.
4. And then why talk of removing poverty in a short period? Even fifty years will not be sufficient {all know}.

5. Things have gone now beyond training of govt. officials {all know}.

Let us be free to comment on the above statements.

My Comments	Your Comments
1. Yes, well known	
2. Yes but due to helplessness {by the time you finish reading this book, you will not feel the same.}	
3. Planning should be introduced as a subject at elementary level onwards to make it a personal habit.	
4. This book shows that it is possible otherwise.	
5. Not true if concepts are simplified and made implemental easily and in a practical way.	

The above shows that we as citizens of India need to change our mindsets and attitudes, first towards poverty and its removal.

As a nation, are we not supposed to provide nutritious food, clothing, housing, employment, and many modern amenities to each person or member of the nation i.e. to everybody in the population? The answer is yes by everybody but the issues are money, high population, resources, will to vanish poverty and by whom. We have discussed each of these in detail in the previous chapters.

We sum up the mindset and attitudinal requirements for the vision of 'Total Removal of Poverty in 5 years' as given below.

1. *Udyogi Mindset:* Innovation, Creativity, Hard Work, and Creation of Wealth.
2. *Mindset of Superlative Adjectives:* Best, Biggest, Longest life, etc.
3. *4 Virtues Mindset:* Hard Work, Honesty, Empathy and Pride.
4. *Positive Attitude:* Think positive all the time and on all matters.

As a nation, the above have to be instilled, nurtured and developed at macro, meso and micro level; providing a holistic approach towards the goal to quick removal of poverty. In nutshell, it works out that each and every citizen–child, young, youth, adult and old, male or female – will need change, will have to be cultivated to have the above mindsets and attitude.

This in itself is a big task to be initiated on war-footing and continuously reinforced for every day of the year, for 5 years and beyond. Education and training across all ages and abilities, for the whole population will have to be set and achieved on continuous basis using all avenues of communication.

Since this aspect of developmental process is so important especially for the vision of total removal of poverty in 5 years, that central government should appoint a minister. The responsibility of the ministry is to be:

1. Public and private agencies to be mobilized to inculcate the *Udyogi Mindset* and other essential features as enumerated earlier; within central and state governments administration, communities, organizations and citizens.
2. To develop a framework for reviewing progress and disseminating the best practices through bi-annual conferences.
3. If a full 5-year plan is made, if hard focus is to be maintained on removal of poverty, many administrative personnel will be redundant in various departments

and sections of government. All of these personnel will have to be used to implement the vision, and some of these personnel are to be used for the purpose of spreading developmental mindsets and attitudes including to existing non-governmental organizations (NGOs) to correctly direct efforts and strengthen social dialogue to find common ground for holistic action. The NGOs specifically for this role also need to be created and innovations and creativity must be promoted in these organisations.

4. Positive examples, role models, activities of *Udyogi Mindset, Mindset of Superlative Adjectives, 4 Virtues and Positive Attitude* are crucial for vanishing poverty from India; to be communicated to citizens.
5. To make this as mainstream, unconscious thought and practice in all spheres of life political or apolitical, administration and as a general public ethos and norms, the best practices within Media and Media to Citizens, are to be honoured and encouraged.
6. The Government policies and actions must initiate, support, strengthen, and encourage the subject mindsets.
7. India is a vast country and at present a sizeable population which does not read or write is there as a matter of fact. It is not feasible to make everyone to do so (read and write) in such a short time and any attempt in this direction of making all read or write fluently in very short period will be a futile exercise. Hence, various communication media will have to be adapted to change and train for skills required in execution of projects.

Anyway, as per the action plans in this book, existing level of education and skills with marginal augmentation will be sufficient for execution of activities to meet the goals.

However, it does not mean that the development of

requisite mindsets and attitudes can be ignored. It must remain as first priority because it will strengthen the society and foundation pillars besides substantial gain in the process of removal of poverty.

8. The normal differentiation of competency and skill levels is not to be forgotten. Competency differentiation is to be based on knowledge, ability to comprehend bigger picture, initiative, pro-activity, independence, innovation, creativity, leadership and delegation. Skills differentiation is to be based on the trained abilities of planning, organizing, managing, analyzing, communicating, de-briefing, evaluation, recording, individual working and team working.
9. Education must imbibe, support and inculcate these mindsets and attitudes at all levels of education–from childhood education to adulthood education. Most of the subjects curriculum and course books will need modification to focus on these mindsets and attitudes. However, immediately, supplementary booklets/books are to be added to the course books/course curriculum to fulfill urgent requirement of getting started on the programme.

Summary

- *'Udyogi' mindset*
- *Mindset of Superlative Adjectives*
- *4 Virtues mindset*
- *Positive Attitude*

— *Government to start a ministry to inculcate the above.*

Nation's apex power centre to initiate the vision 'Removal of Poverty in 5 Years'. This will make also a Richer India in a short span of time.

Chapter - 15

Action List – Individual Level

Trees of flowers and fruits give immense satisfaction to human beings. Those who plant and donate such trees, receive blessings of happiness of the other world, trees are like sons.

— Mahabharata

Assist in creating conducive environment

1. Be sensitive to sight of poverty.
2. Never vote for a political party (or a candidate) which tries to exploit natural familiar sentiments of have-nots using regional or linguistic or religious or caste issues.
3. Refuse to mentally accept anything and everything as fate. Be a *Karmayogi*. It does not mean to fight or quarrel on every injustice happening to you but do not give up mentally.
4. One must take extra care to avoid wastage of any food items and drinking water.
5. One must take extra care not to spoil, waste, deface or destroy national wealth.
6. One must take care to keep the surroundings, environment, places of habitat or work, roads and cities or villages neat, clean and green.

Assist in creating national wealth

7. Last but most important, whatever one does, must do with utmost sincerity and of best quality. One must

think big to create the best in the world, "Creation of good quality National Wealth" must always be the motto. Nation must come first, all other considerations are secondary.

8. Every individual must plant and tender at least five fruit trees of long life variety - two for parents, two for children and one for spouse. It is not necessary that the fruit trees have to be on his/her land only - no, it can be anywhere, considering some living beings, some human beings, some children will eat the fruits one day. The trees may feed a hungry child someday.

Assist in creating equitable and inclusive distribution process

9. Understand value of your country's currency and try to enhance the value. This will help in better distribution process.

10. Refuse to overpay for a commodity or item of daily use. One might need to sacrifice little bit of immediate need fulfillment. If some start to buy at higher prices, retailers and middlemen start charging more in general and to all citizens. This hurts those who can not afford to buy at that price. This small alertness and a little sacrifice in short term on the part of individuals will check inflation, correct quality and will be a very effective tool for more equitable and inclusive distribution process. Bad distribution process in a nation creates many poor though availability on national level may be there for all citizens.

11. Do not fall prey to logic of middlemen and retailers to have few customers at higher prices, which is practiced for higher profits with less efforts. They do not care even if there are wastages. But any wastage is loss of national wealth and also wastage of the efforts of those who created the items.

12. Move away from the "tip giving" culture. Yes, one may get better service next time. But it hurts more to general public. Salary for service of the waiters/service providers to be inclusive of income coming from tips and it may be included in the items' price. Always remember that the time you do not have the extra money to give tip, you will get bad service next time. Tip culture spoils and degenerates the services sector. It adversely affects the social fabrics.

13. It is important to de-criminalize the national society. Crimes can not be totally eliminated, but definitely can be reduced to a great extent. Reduction of crimes is absolute necessity to eliminate fear in individuals and also for equitable and inclusive distribution process for basic goods and services.

—Do not be a party to increase of salaries and wages beyond the average inflation rate and for some individuals small percentage for performance credit. High salary rise for performance will lead to cheating in the system. Definitely bring down the managerial wages/salaries if within your authority area. Higher wages help no body, including the person who gets it, in the proportion of rise. But the worst sufferer are the poor people, a majority today, if some small section of the population gets much higher wages, salaries or profit. It affects the desired equitable and inclusive distribution process of the nation.

[Always remember, who falls in haves and have-not categories on this earth is only due to chance. If have-nots snatch by force, haves will loose; so never aid towards such a situation to crystallize. Democracy is better for freedom of individuals.]

—Help in de-criminalizing the politics—by not voting or supporting those who are known for their unsocial activities. Many say that they vote for the party and not for individuals. The times have changed, the times have arrived, that vote must be given in favour of only those candidates having clean records; this is absolutely necessary irrespective of the political party affiliation of the candidates. This will force the political parties to put up clean candidates.

—Help in de-criminalizing of politics—by not voting for those who have generated unaccounted or too fast personal wealth in a short period.

—Look down upon those individuals who have amassed personal wealth or power by unfair means. This is necessary to break the nexus of politicians, criminals and industrialists. This nexus will always try to expand and continue for the reason of getting the higher benefits. To some extent it is ok, but beyond a point, it subverts the equitable and inclusive distribution process, it hampers distribution of basic items of food, clothing and shelters to rest of the population of a nation or state.

Lastly,

—Follow and help in creating developmental mindsets and attitudes.

Chapter - 16

Action List – Community Level/Social/Industrial Organizations

We live in a moment of history where change is so speeded up that we begin to see the present only when it is already disappearing.

— RD Laing *"The Politics of Experience"*

Assist in creating conducive environment

1. For any decision to be made, weigh the decision also in the backdrop of national interest. If it is not in national interest, just do not succumb to factional/regional/linguistic/religious or quick and excessive profit considerations and totally avoid that decision. This process will bring harmony in the society, which is essential for removing poverty.
2. Create social awareness for good values, mindsets and attitudes necessary to expedite removal of poverty by creation of wealth and equitable all inclusive distribution.
3. Avoid aping the western culture in all aspects of society and life. Except valueing the science, technological and engineering developments of western society and culture; and trying to emulate the development environment for cultivation of the same, there is nothing more to emulate. Rest of the culture for them is developed under very icy cold environment and

shortage/pressure of food availability. Their financial systems, their medical service systems, their social norms and mores, their religions are not conducive to happiness of individuals in the long range and should be avoided to be copied. It will be better to develop your country systems seamlessly merging with your natural environments.

But always be humble and open to fresh ideas in any field from anybody. India suffered due to arrogance of Indians in the medieval period.

4. Whatever is mentioned in the chapter "Action List – Individuals", the organizations need to make individuals aware about, cultivate and help individuals to follow the same.

Assist in creating national wealth

5. Communities to create co-operatives for planting fruit trees on barren lands and hills. Social organizations to cooperate and guide for planting of long life fruit trees in urban areas, on the sides of the roads, in parks, in townships, near hills, villages and in front of village houses. Other organizations must ensure that their own vacant land is planted with long and medium life fruit trees. Many organizations will have persons to counteract that they are not in the business of fruit tree plantations and selling fruit trees and monkeys will come, etc. When children are hungry, when children are malnourished, when future citizens of a country are going to be hungry, when future of a nation is hanging on food availability; every body is in the business of food production besides their own primary business, besides their own call of duty and such petty arguments to be overcome amicably. Distribute the fruits to the employees, they will be happy.

6. Social organizations guide and assist in planning for wide roads, super large parks for vegetable and fruits cultivation within residential communities, fruit and vegetable vendor shelters just like bus stands or part of the bus stands on the sides of the roads, biodiversity parks, large and world's best museums, waste management sites etc in urban areas of cities and townships.
7. Social organizations guide and assist in smooth development of canals and joining of rivers by governments.
8. Community Organizations, industries and housing societies with reasonably big gardens to plant long, medium, and short life fruit trees – like pomegranate, drumstick, cheeku, orange, karondha, aonla, etc. instead of ornamental trees. Similarly, instead of grass lawns, plan for vegetable lawns. The arguments of who will eat, definitely must be kept aside, otherwise nothing will happen. Let someone eat, but at national level production of fruits and vegetables goes up. For some it will be patriotic sacrifice and for some small gifts from the society and nation.

Assist in creating equitable and inclusive distribution process

9. Create awareness to de-criminalize the society and social fabric made of various agencies and segments.
10. Create outlets for food items and clothings and building/ house materials on 'no loss no profit' philosophy.

Chapter - 17

Action List–Government Level

President means Chief Servant.

—M K Gandhi

	Activity	Time Days
1.	Declaration of commitment to "Removal of Poverty in 5 Years" vision.	Start
2.	Communication to the nation that rapid employment generation will automatically happen under the programme 'Removal of Poverty in 5 Years.	Start
3.	Legislation to stop/prohibit exports of any food items whether raw or processed including food supplements like milk and milk products, meat, poultry, eggs, fish, fruits, vegetables, etc., for the next 20 years.	30-90
4.	Legislation to stop/prohibit exports of any low/medium quality clothing material and building materials used in creation of dwellings, residences, housings, office buildings, etc. These exports to be barred at least for the next 20 years.	30-150
5.	Legislation to stop/prohibit exports of any raw materials like iron ore, other metal ores,	30-180

coal, mica, etc., for ever. This will bring pressures to export only finished engineering goods and curtail the imports of goods similar to already manufactured inside the country. What is the fun in importing a luxury car costing Rs. 2 crore when some have to sweat to earn the required foreign exchange without even getting proper food and drinking water, clothing and decent housing? This legislation will be construed as going back on liberalization, but in long term immense benefits for the nation will be derived. (*Judicious imports are necessary and must happen).* But injudicious imports are throwing away the national wealth for status symbol of some individuals.

6. Every employment to be evaluated against 30-180
the backdrop of creation and distribution of National Wealth. Example, stock market operators do not add any wealth creation for the nation. FDI (foreign direct investment) do not create any national wealth if these only operate at stock exchange level; however in opening of a manufacturing unit or a production unit, these do bring in fresh ideas and technology, hence limited encouragement may be appropriate.

   But again in service sector, a nation should not touch the same with even a long pole, since all the miseries of their own services will also be presented as virtues and any way that does not add any national wealth. Example—medical insurance.

Even in manufacturing/production sector, one has to be careful of the intentions. Enron case is still vivid,they spent hundreds of crore to educate the political class which was nothing but corruption with another name and ran away with the national wealth, in essence of other goods created by Indian citizens and exported for earning the foreign exchange.

7. All forms of government direct or indirect subsidies whether physical or notional must be withdrawn except in the domains of food and food related production and distribution, certain types of clothing materials, and building raw materials for housings, dwellings, residences. 30-90

8. Carpet area of flats, residences, dwellings, houses, is to be minimum of 100 sq. m. (1000 sq. ft.) from an effective date onwards. [New York state in USA specifies the maximum grass height in lawns around a house, otherwise prosecution/penalty for the owner. Besides good look of the environment, this has definitely helped the health of residents since they have to cut the grass every week and the machine is heavy and pushed or pulled manually]. 100

   Nowadays small rooms flats being built by builders and sold at exorbitant prices beyond the reach of the common man, will kill the human spirit for very long periods of 30 to 100 years in future for the citizens. {Sound mind in healthy body in spacious environment will only create best quality national wealth}

9. Introduce Maximum Salary Norm (inclusive of perks) as 50 times of the median income per citizen for the nation. Industrialists earn huge amounts as dividend on their equity in the industry and it is tax free; hence it will not affect the general environment for the development of industries. But this legislation will provide immediate and long term impact on enhancing the value of currency, which in turn will help in equitable and inclusive distribution of the basic goods to very large segment of the population of the nation. 30-90

   It will check inflation; will lead to negative inflation; which is the purpose. It will enhance industrial growth in the long range since labour costs, as well as costs all around will go down in real terms.

   If 50 times works out to less, it could be more but there has to be a limit. Fifty percent of population earns below median income and 50 times of that earning has to be satisfying for every man. Under no circumstances the man earning that is 50 times better than the man earning median income.

10. 6 months training programme for all elected members of the governmental set-up. 100

11. Performance evaluation system to be rolled out for all elected members who get into governance. 100

12. Governance towards decriminalizing of politics, break-up of nexus of politicians-criminals-industrialists. 30-180

- Immediate discontinuation of development funds allocation to MPs and MLAs and Corporators.
- Discontinuance of life long benefits to them for the next 30 years.

The above will move the criminals out of politics, leading to equitable and inclusive politics. Which other jobs pay life long for 5 years of service? {This will be resisted tooth and nails in a democratic setup, but if not done, the next generation of politicians may not be there to form the governments. But nation will be a great looser. The applaud of general public for the party which succeeds in doing this will be great and will be remembered for cleaning the politics.}

13. Communication to citizens through various media regarding the mindsets and attitudes necessary for development and for the implementation of vision "Removal of Poverty in 5 Years". *
14. Severe punishments to be legislated for cheating, food adulteration, using government facilities or subsidies for purposes other than intended. Its implementations to be quick, final judgments from all courts coming out within a year and start of punishment within a year. 100
15. Change in constitution is required. A citizen can be elected only for two terms to Lok Sabha or Rajya Sabha or State Assembly. The country must get fresh people to represent and govern. India has suffered too long (for 60 years) and with the same 180

faces, its only old wine in a new bottle (new 5 years term).

Creating Conducive Environment

1. Process of bringing more rational exchange 300
rates must be initiated. Gradually but quickly exchange rates must reach to purchasing power parity rates. Example 1 $ = Rs. 10 or Rs. 12. Otherwise every export and import to developed nations is loss to India and subsidy to the developed nation.And then, bring gradually the parity in exchange rate that is as close to one as feasible for the currencies of developed nations.

2. To make politicians also good politicians 100
(today the worst social examples), first and foremost, no government security to be provided to anybody except the president, prime minister, state chief ministers, and Chief Justices of supreme court and high courts.

   Even ministers do not need the government security. Senior officers in industries do not move with government security, though they deal with more aggressive labour and their dealings are much more intense than the government officials and functionaries. Do Tatas, Birlas, and Ambanis move with government security? Then why an MP, MLA, or even a sundry politician not having won an election gets government security. Politicians are using the government security to indulge in unlawful activities, intimidate other peaceful citizens for gains and incite others; they being protected on citizens resources.

When this protection will be removed, there will be molestations and murders of some politicians by some politicians to show that the protection is necessary. But once they learn that it is not going to be re-provided, then there will be lasting calm. Hence the uprising incidents to be ignored and this protection be summarily removed.

The most of the government security provided for individuals is for either prestige or for doing *gundagiri* using the government and citizen's resources. There is no solution for India, unless this facility is withdrawn in one go.

3. Adulteration of food items and medicines is to be treated on par with mass murder crime and capital punishment only to be provisioned. All adulteration cases to be summarily decided within 3 months. 100

4. The governments to start ministry to inculcate Developmental Mindsets and Attitudes. 100

5. Governments to start ministry of Standardization and Catalogs. 100

Creating Equitable Inclusive Distribution Process

1. Remove all subsidies except on food, certain items of clothing and certain items of housing. 200

   (Fuel Oil subsidy alone during 2008-09 was Rs. 1,03,000 crore)

2. Basic food items prices to be reduced to very nominal level in the open market. The

prices become applicable to all citizens—it saves resources from following procedures, implementation, control, etc. It will be simple, effective, and free from corruption and does not make much difference in subsidy requirements. Also it will have salutary positive effect on overall value of currency and national environment for growth.

This is the best method of equitable and inclusive distribution.

Wheat	– Rs. 2/kg
Rice	– Rs. 2/kg.
All Dal varieties	– Rs. 2/kg.
Onions	– Rs. 3/kg
Potatoes	– Rs. 3/kg.
All vegetables	– Rs. 3/kg.
Fruits	– Rs. 4/kg.
Milk	– Rs. 2/liter.

Benefits of the above action have been discussed in the earlier chapters. If all other subsidies are removed, this is easily feasible.

3. Stop waste of resources in identifying the poor, or persons below the poverty line. Presently in India, except a very small percentage of citizens (less than 10%), all are poor. There is no point in arguing about definition of poor. 60

4. A clothing material (with different colours and prints) for men in open market: @ Rs. 2/meter 200

5. A clothing material (with different colors and prints) for women in open market: @ Rs. 2/meter. 100
6. A house for family to be available @ Rs. 1.8 Lac. 900
7. Children up to the age of 12 to be provided with free food at schools. Food besides normal grains items must have at least 100 grams of fresh seasonal fruits, 100 ml of milk and 50 grams of jaggary mixed with vegetarian protein every day. 100

Creating National Wealth

Food (For domestic consumption by citizens)

1. Foodgrains availability: 690 gm/capita/day, 10% annual growth. (Foodgrains export for 2007-08 was 97 lakh metric tons, 4.7% of production) 1500
2. Vegetables availability: 400 gm/capita/day 900
3. Fruits availability: 300 gm/capita/day 600
4. Dairy availability: 400 gm/capita/day 900

Clothing

1. One variety availability for all men: 20 meter/male citizen/year 600
2. One variety availability for all women: 20 meter/female citizen/year 300

Housing

- 25 sq. m (250 sq. ft.) carpet area housing per citizen availability 1000

{100 m (1000 sq. ft) carpet area housing for a family}

Infrastructure Projects (New)

1.	Townships on barren lands: 5000 townships of 300000 persons capacity each.	1500
2.	Roads: 1000000 km (15000 km on river banks).	1500
3.	Airports: 6000 nos.	2000
4.	Dredging of rivers: 100000 km.	2000
5.	River Banks: 100000 km.	1500
6.	Water Canals: 100000 km.	1800
7.	Lakes 70m 300m 10m depth - 4000 nos.	600
8.	Lakes 100m 500m 10m depth - 3000 nos.	900
9.	Lakes 150m 800m 15m depth - 2000 nos.	1200
10.	Lakes 200m 1000m 20m depth - 1000 nos.	1500
11.	Rivers Interconnections-100 nos.	1500
12.	Railway Lines: 100000 km.	1500
13.	Space Satellites: 1000 nos.	1800
14.	Missiles: 25000 nos.	1800
15.	Bio Diversity Sanctuaries of minimum 20 sq. km: 10000 nos.	2000
16.	Primary Schools and buildings: 5.3 lac numbers.	900
17.	Middle Schools and buildings: 3.3 lac numbers.	1200
18.	Higher colleges and buildings: 1.35 lac numbers.	1500
19.	Universities/institutions including buildings: 9640 nos.	1800

20. Vocational Technical Training Centers: 99000 nos. 600
21. Underground Shelters (Nuclear Protection): 10000 nos. 1800
22. Museums: 2000 nos. 1800
23. Stadiums: 500 nos. 1200
24. Train Bogies: 30000 nos. 1500
25. Transport Aeroplanes: 5000 nos. 1800
26. Fighter Planes: 10000 nos. 1500
27. Ships: 5000 nos. 1800
28. Nuclear Submarines: 500 nos. 1800
29. Battle Tanks: 50000 nos. 1800
30. Railway Stations: 3000 nos. 1800
31. Super Computers: 1 000 nos. 1500

R&D Projects (target 5 years time line)

1. Research Institutes specifically dedicated to each type of foodgrains in every state and UT.
2. Research Institutes specifically dedicated to each type of vegetable in every state and UT.
3. Research Institutes specifically dedicated to each type of fruit in every state and UT.
4. Research Institutes specifically dedicated to building technology in every state and UT.
5. Research Institutes specifically dedicated to waste management technologies in every state and UT.
6. Manned Moon Centers/Bases: 10 nos.
7. New Antarctica Bases (100 men each): 10 nos.
8. Sea Bases (Mineral Mining Centers): 20 nos.
9. Reusable Space Shuttle: 5 nos.

10. Extreme High Resolution Photographic Capability Satellites: 10 nos.
11. Miniature Nuclear Engines for satellites: 50 nos.
12. Miniature Nuclear Engines for use in air, surface and sea transportation: 100 nos.
13. Sea Bottom Military Bases

    (100 men each): 100 bases along sea shore.
14. Robot soldiers for various tasks at border: 1000 nos.
15. Ultra light tougher than steel material specific gravity. 0.5 gm/cc
16. Cable-less electric power transmission.
17. Missile defence system.
18. Personal flying contraption.
19. One month cultivatable wheat, rice and pulses crops.
20. Nuclear powered missile having 25000 km range 1 m accuracy and 2 ton payload in one hour to any point on earth.
21. Brain cells using stem cells for super computers with nutrients supply system.
22. Skin cells using stem cells for bullet proof skins for secondary clothing for humans.
23. Demonstration of replication of technologies used by nature for giving specific quality/power to various animals, birds and insects.

Appendix - I

AGRICULTURE/FOOD SECURITY

There is no end to innovating the transformations in our future crop varieties/hybrids but it is important to look for our own indigenous gene constructs and promoters so as to be self-dependent and cost-effective in the wake of strong global IPR regimes. Incidentally, the onus lies on the public sector institutions, which undertake most of the transgenic research in India.

...it will be highly important to evolve a scientific and globally acceptable system of deregulation of bio-safe 'events'. ...the agricultural scientific community resolves to intensify the search for new genes and harness the genic power to enhance agricultural productivity, profitability.

—Mangal Rai, Secretary, (DARE) &
DirectorGeneral, ICAR;

12th Dr B P Pal Memorial Lecture, 2009

Agriculture is one area which needs fresh thinking, paradigm shift, new development model, reengineering, new research and new technology, different distribution model, long term planning, and even a new national development index on yesterday's priority.

What is the real measure of national development? A national development index, a one item, should reflect the total picture of status of the nation's citizens.

There is one ratio, which as an index, shows all about a nation's scenario, status of its citizens, how poor or rich the citizens are, what is their health status, and how much discretionary income is available with them for other pursuits. The proposed index below gives insight of a nation's progress. It is simple and easy. May it be said that rest all indices for a nation's progress are only gimmicks and camouflage.

$$\text{National Development Index} = \frac{\text{Food Expenditure per capita for balanced nutritious food (Unit Rs./month)}}{\text{Median Income per capita (Unit Rs./month)}}$$

Why food expenditure per capita for balanced nutritious food? Because, the actual expenditure may not be reflecting the real scenario. There may be shortage of some items or there may be very high price for some items and it may not be in the buying baskets of the general public. Not only that, some governments cheat their own citizens by showing huge availability but the price is so high that people reduce the consumption to meet household budget. But the item may be an absolute necessity for good health. In India the current example for few years have been the edible oils and pulses and recently sugar, garlic, ginger, vegetables, etc., have been added to this ever expanding list.

Average versus Median Income

Why median income per capita and not average income per capita? This is because average income can be very deceptive. Just to understand this, a numerical example is being cited.

We take eleven persons' monthly income as given below:

500000, 15000, 8000, 4000, 2000, 2000, 2000, 1000, 500, 0, 0

The average income per month per capita (for the 11 persons example)

= Rs. 534500/11

= Rs. 48590/-

The distortion in the average figure is so obvious. One person (may be managing director of a small company) earning high income is pulling the average figure upward, showing average of Rs. 48590/- per month. The other 10 persons are earning nowhere near the average; they are all earning much lower income. So though average shows that all the 11 can easily afford food, but in reality only one person can afford nutritious healthy food and two persons of the lot have to die of hunger. Indian present scenario is exactly similar to this example.

To overcome the above anomaly, median should be taken. Median is the central value of the data, if the values of the data are arranged in ascending or descending order. Thus median divides the total frequency into two equal parts.

The median monthly income for the 11 persons example (the sixth value in this case) = Rs. 2000/-

Though this is also not giving completely true picture in the sense that one person is very rich and can afford whatever he wishes to eat or buy, and 2 persons have to go hungry since they do not have any purchasing power, but it is much closer to reality: for most persons income is low and healthy food is difficult to afford. Immediately question arises that affordability depends on the food prices and the upper term of NDI is trying to figure out that. Overall this index gives much better real picture.

Now what is per capita? This is nothing but 'per citizen of the total population'.

Some governments try to manipulate general public by taking only households, some governments try to mislead by taking only that population which is in working age group. These are not real indicator of the status. After all food and clothing are required by everybody whether man or woman, young or old and not only by those who are in the working age group. Hence, to present and understand the actual state of affairs, it is necessary to take every citizen of the country i.e., total population.

The international organizations like World Bank rely more on GDP, GNP per capita, or on GNI. These are average figures and do not represent the picture correctly.

India, it seems officially does not calculate the above especially the requirement for food, and the median income per capita. Probably the reason is that the Median Income for the whole of India is so low that it is shameful after 60 years of independence.

The average per capita income in India for 2008-09 was mere Rs. 3345 per month at the 2008-09 prices. For Madhya Pradesh, U.P. and Bihar the average per capita income per month in 2008-09 at 2008-09 prices was Rs. 1047/-, Rs. 886/-, Rs. 551/- respectively. Is there food affordability/ availability today or tomorrow? Passing legislation for food security is not going to make the food affordable or available all over India. It needs different type of actions and different focus or a different new model of development, a paradigm shift to make it happen.

Credibility of Data is Important in Decision Making

It is also important to maintain credibility of data and availability of latest data for meaningful managerial decisions. It is government's responsibility to support collection of systematically correct data, analysis of data, and make it available to one and all. Today, the situation is pathetic. The web sites of these government agencies put data which are decades old and of low relevance. In modern days collection and use of data is considered most important to guide decision making. The bureaucracy, if they do not have the required data, how can they make correct decisions?

It is also important that, ruling political party should not demand, and the bureaucracy should never agree for manipulation of collected data. It is very easy to fall prey or get tempted to manipulate data for public consumption and for short term gains. But this harms the whole nation and should be a punishable offence. At the end, it even harms the political party due to loss of credibility. The government's claim of poor household after NSS 55th (2002) was that 27.7% of households in India are poor and it was used for Plan 2002-2007. But reality was very different. Example : After a survey of some villages in West Bengal and presented in a paper by Neela Mukhherjee at Manchester on 25 November 2005 during the International Conference *'Redesigning the State? Political Corruption in Development Policy and Practice,'* the paper shows that average of 71% of households (in some villages over 90%) were poor with the similar criterion. In rural India, all know the inadequacies of BPL households finalizations based on that survey by NSS and still being used since new survey has yet to be made. The Government lost the credibility of data.

A few words regarding the food prices

(a) Logic is being put forward by some vested interests that higher retail prices of food now are going to bring higher benefits to the farmers.

This is absurd in concept, absurd in spirit and absurd in logic and far away from reality. First, do the higher retail food prices ensure more payment to the farmers? No, since mostly it benefits the middlemen, the real estate owners, and business politicians. Farmers do not get even a fraction of the additional rise in price. If at all farmers get anything, it is very small percentage of the actual retail food price rise. It is absurd in concept.

Second, higher fooa prices trigger higher prices for everything else. It benefits only few and creates arduous grilling for rest of the population. It is bad in spirit.

Third, India has mostly small farmers. Agricultural land is divided in many small family holdings. The surplus grains normally come from very large farmers. Small farmer may sell small quantity of one or two items to get some cash to buy food items other than what he grows. This list is much bigger than what he produced. Now, since the food prices have gone up, he has to pay more for every other food item. Also for other items of necessity which the small farmer has to buy to run the small farm and family, he has to pay more. At the end, the small farmer ends paying much more than what he gained. And since he has no money, he goes hungry, in some acute cases, the farmer commits suicide. If the food prices go up, there will be more distress to the farming community in general in India.

(b) Food prices converted in other currencies is most misleading and to be never, never used. This acute distortion comes due to distortion in the exchange rate. If food prices are converted to dollar or euro or British pound, every item in India will seem to be at throw away prices when compared to the prices in USA or Europe or United Kingdom. It is solely because of the exchange rate regime created and operated by these countries for their own benefits. When the food items price is compared in those currencies, one must also look at those countries median income per capita in their own currency. And then it is an eye opener. In India food is unimaginably expensive for its own citizens. The citizens of those countries get food at throwaway prices and they do throw and waste which a common citizen in India can not even imagine.

(c) Public policy of making food available at nominal prices is responsibility of governments and they cannot absolve of the same.

The above brings to the subject started in the beginning of this chapter. The National Development Index (NDI) proposed at the beginning of this chapter in percentage terms has to be found out for India. Presently, it may turn out to be 150% or 200% or even 300%; actual will definitely be more than 100% i.e. most of the Indian population is undernourished and cannot afford food required for good health.

The Central Government jointly with state governments has to finalize what percentage figure is achievable in the next 5 years, next 10 years, next 15 years and 20 years. If India reaches a figure of even 50% in 5 years, it will be really commendable.

What will be the desired figure of the Index? The desired figure has to be very low, 10%. The government must concentrate and put a target of bringing the food expenditure to 10% of national median income per capita. The developed countries have achieved close to this figure and some advanced countries have been able to achieve even lower than 10%. For India it will be a far cry but let all work to achieve this goal and then country will have really progressed; a real inclusive development.

The 10% is the desired figure to cover all those who are below the median income. Fifty per cent of population earns below the median figure, the variation in earning is large and population at the bottom of the descending array is in most distress. Nutritional needs are sacrificed by these have-nots whose earnings are below the median figure and government agencies must research and develop public policies to overcome the malady. Sustainable development is possible only when the nutritional requirements of this class of society is taken care of; then only the future generations who are children today will be capable to sustain and build the nation.

Let one more premise be clear to one and all, being told here at the cost of repetition : The process of providing *roti, kapda aur makan* to all citizens, takes care of *sadak, bijli aur pani.* The two are closely interrelated and discussed in previous chapters.

Next is a pyramid of national food availability showing what is actually ingested by individuals. This pyramid shows the pitfalls of just looking at any data for food availability. Nation has to be careful in projecting the status on food availability by clearly looking and absorbing at which portion of the pyramid is being referred to.

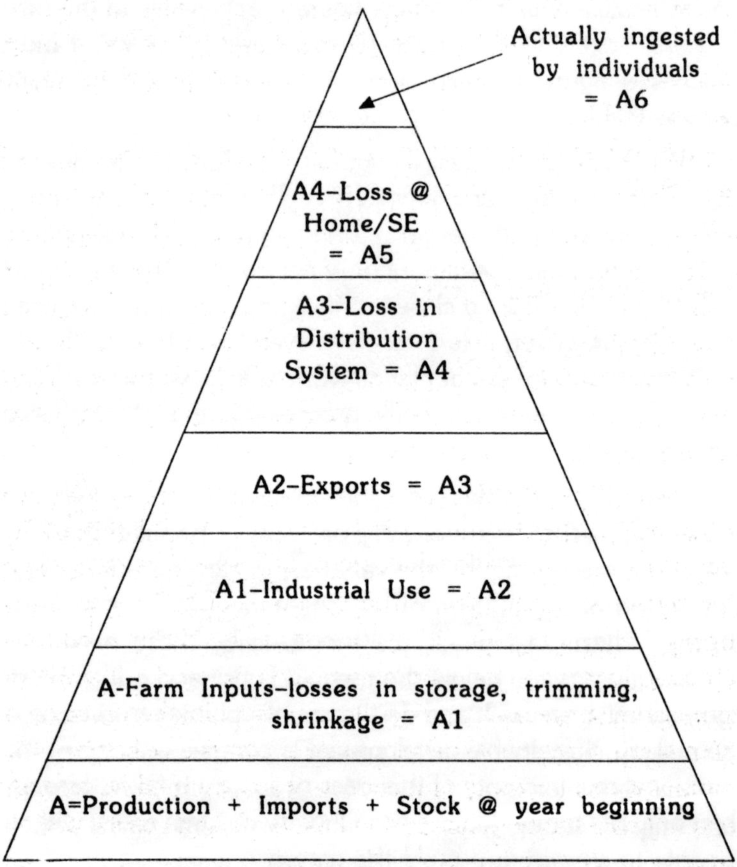

Central Statistical Organization (CSO) has to properly collect data and generate data for A6 on annual basis to understand real availability to the citizens. The subject pyramid should be generated for each food item and then for each group of food items like grains, sweeteners, meats, poultry, fisheries, vegetables, fruits etc, and of course at aggregate level.

How to increase A6 portion starting from A portion? Each step to be analyzed and actions will need to be taken to increase A6 i.e. finally eaten by the citizens and which provides the required nutrition.

It has been experienced that healthy effect of good nutrition on individuals is best when there is availability of clean drinking water. The two go hand in hand or one after another in the mouth. While planning for food availability, clean drinking water availability must be planned simultaneously as an integrated plan.

Genetically Modified Crop

There is a lobby, fuelled by external, out of country profit oriented organizations, to go for genetically modified agricultural and other food items like Bt Brinjal, or GM fruits or GM grains. These organizations are trying to take the bogey of food shortage, less growth in food production and many such arguments to get foothold. Ultimate aim is not human service but profit and anti-national elements will always be available to bat these organizations. If the country is not careful, it will bring hegemony like the foreign rule earlier. Without independent, very long term, repeated research, these food items should not be let inside the country, whether in open or clandestine form. Really speaking these associations/ organisations for food items which are consumed by humans and animals should be in banned list for foreign participation, foreign equity and foreign collaboration. It will be wrong to say that we should not keep our eyes open for technology in this field, but let it be 110 % indigenous research and technology.

There are many reasons for stagnation in agricultural production or growth in agriculture and other food items. One of them is the basic input of production—land, to be more specific arable land or fertile land. There is severe loss of arable land to Estate Developers, SEZ, and Industries. There are certain sections of society, though small in number, who are, by distortion in distribution process, are able to corner resources and then human greed is fuelling land grabbing. Public policy urgently needs course correction so as the land available for food production does not go for any other purpose; irrespective of the land's location or reasonableness of the non-agricultural demand. Employment of a person without food is as good as no employment.

Ministry of Food Availability

Agriculture, for its meaning, is limited and does not indicate the actual objective a minister should focus on. The ministry should be redesigned as 'Ministry of Food Availability' or 'Ministry of Food Security' to convey the real objective. It should deal with all aspects of food production (agricultural production, vegetable production, fruit production, dairy, poultry, fisheries, meat production), food imports if necessary, distribution keeping in view the individual nutrient requirements, clean drinking water availability.

The planning process in this ministry should have minimum perspective of 20 years with development of rolling plan for the next 20 years. For example if exports of food items have to be banned, it should be banned for at least 20 years. Independent research needs to be done for genetically modified seeds and crops for the next 20 years to see the long term effects on humans before introduction.

It's ironic and myopic if an incumbent in this ministry thinks his responsibility is only for farmers' interest. Actually if he takes care of all citizens, he has also taken care of the farmers. At the end, from administration point of view and for expediency of actions, this ministry is too big and should have many ministers of state, each handling one of the verticals like, agriculture, vegetable, fruit, meat, poultry, fisheries, clean drinking water, etc. This ministry needs to be managed on the lines of a very large manufacturing organization.

Some of the do's for food availability

(i) *Feverish actions for increasing land area in cultivation.*

(ii) *Ban on use of agricultural land for any other purpose and nobody, no agency, no government is authorized to allow conversion of agricultural land to non-agricultural use. Even take away a land permitted earlier but not yet in use fully or partially from other use to agricultural use i.e. for cultivation.*

(iii) *Conversion of barren land to arable or productive land.*

(iv) *Increase incentives for better productivity in all areas of food production except food processing industries.*

(v) *Direct incentives for use of natural manure.*

(vi) *Create multi-storied mechanized cow and buffalo farms in the cities for dairy.*

(vii) *Ban exports of food items and of inputs of food production.*

(viii) *Subsidize food for all (not only poor families because it gets looted before it reaches). It is small cost compared to total budget and lower prices are the best means of ensuring inclusive distribution.*

(ix) *Encourage indigenous research for genetically modified seeds and crops. Effectively ban all foreign associations in this sensitive area.*

(x) *Central and state administration to be reengineered for food availability.*

(xi) *Make it mandatory to grow vegetables over the top of buildings by creating light weight large size plastic containers having thin layer of soil in all metros, cities and towns. It is just to bring culture of production of food items on war footing and to make aware to city dwellers that food production is focused activity and precious.*

(xii) *Fruit trees plantation is to be declared a national activity.*

(xiii) *Adulteration of food items to be equated equal to mass murder and death penalty to be legislated on top most priority.*

Summary

- *Ministry of Agriculture to reinvent itself as Ministry of Food Availability and Security.*
- *Urgent actions are needed as given above.*
- *Percentage of agriculture or food related activities-may go down in overall GDP; but its importance, the government's focus on this, the torch light has to remain all the time on this aspect and major portion of expenditure allocation (in other terms resource allocation) in the annual budget and projections for long terms, must always be made on food availability.*
- *Food items prices to be very nominal for all citizens, best method for equitable and inclusive distribution.*

$$\text{National Development Index} = \frac{\text{Food expenditure per capita for balanced nutritious food (Unit Rs./month)}}{\text{Median Income per capita (Unit Rs./month)}}$$

Appendix - II

FRUITS AND FRUIT TREES

In barren tracts of the country, there shall be constructed not only tanks, buildings for shelter, and wells, but also flower gardens and FRUIT GARDENS

— *Arthashastra* by Kautilya,

Book II – The duties of Government Superintendents, Chapter xxxiv – The Superintendent of Passports.

- **If hunger has to be vanished, planting fruit trees 'is the solution'.**
- **If global warming has to be controlled, planting fruit trees 'is the solution'.**

The potential outcome of large scale fruit free plantation is so high, that a full chapter needs to be devoted on this subject. It is important that each and every citizen of India should and must know about fruit trees to some extent as general knowledge. Every citizen will have to be involved in planting fruit trees. 'Fruit Trees' must be a part of educational curriculum every year of education from primary to graduation.

Advantages of Fruit Trees

1. **Alleviates Hunger:** Normally, beneficiary citizens are those who are consuming the fruits. But all citizens must consume fruits, in the process, releasing foodgrains also for all citizens.

2. **Alleviates Poverty:** Availability of food for all citizens is one of the measures of eliminating poverty. Fruits availability

in plenty will do that. However, fruit tree saplings creation, planting fruit trees, maintaining plantations, harvesting fruits, distribution channels for fruits and its preparations, manufacturing of fruits base food items, providing manure, water, herbal pesticides etc. will create huge employment opportunities, more for rural/tribal employment, but also for the urban employment in the supporting roles, supporting industries.

3. **Alleviates malnourished/undernourished**: Even modern medical researches have shown that consumption of fruits on daily basis and in good quantity is absolutely necessary for human body and mind growth and maintenance. Consumption of fruits on daily basis makes a person disease-free including cancer and heart diseases. If the future generations of Indians have to be strong, intelligent, and physically and mentally fit; large scale plantation of fruit trees is an absolute must. Every citizen of India must plant at least one fruit tree for each of his/her child. This is minimum one can do for the future generation.

4. **Reduces medical expenditure/health care resource requirements**: Fruits are normally rich in vitamins and minerals essential for good health. Hence, less visits to doctors and hospitals.

5. **Reduces Global Warming**: Trees and plants have two basic processes just like us– breathing and consumption of food. For breathing, trees and plants, again just like us, take oxygen and expel carbon dioxide. But for food making process it is reverse, unlike ours, intake is carbon dioxide and expel oxygen. Oxygen is necessary for human survival (all animals and plants life, moving and stationary life). Excess production of carbon dioxide is responsible in raising the average temperature on our planet earth. The trees and plants food making process is very valuable for maintaining the balance on our planet earth. Trees have to make more food during "fruiting". Just like pregnant ladies, fruit trees need more food during "fruiting". This means consumption of more carbon

dioxide by the tree and consequently more effective reduction in Global Warming.

6. **Employment generation:** Fruits tree plantation and fruits distribution and fruits processing will generate both rural/ tribal as well as urban employment. Also the employment will be equitable and pervading all over this vast country.

7. **Savings in Fuel (cooking gas)/energy:** Since most of the fruits are eaten raw, there is virtual savings in fuel consumption/energy consumption. If fruits will not be there, only grains and vegetables are consumed, there will be requirement for fuel (cooking gas) or energy (electrical etc.) for the additional grains consumed.

8. **Production of Bio-Manure:** When fruits are eaten, there generates good amount of bio wastage – covering, seeds etc. Take example of oranges– juice is consumed but rest of the fruit material is thrown as a waste. Most of the fruit consumption generates waste.

If this waste is collected (and it is definitely feasible if there is a national will to do the same) and processed as a Bio-Manure, it will be helping in reduction of the synthetic fertilizers use. Consequently, this will help in improving the health of citizens.

9. **Leaves Powder Industry:** At present most of the leaves are either burnt in the forest or it rots all the places. If leaves are collected, powdered and formed to make biodegradable containers on the mass scale, it will get recycled and during the intermediate stage, people have usable items. Example pots in the plant nurseries instead of plastic bags. Containers to throw waste material during/after fruit eating in the households/fruit shops and then the containers along with the fruit wastage is collected and processed for making Bio-Manure. In a tropical country like India this has a big potential.

10. **Medical Use:** Most of the fruit tree's bark, leaves, seeds are used for making medicines for curing wounds, and various diseases by tribals. Ayurveda uses plants and its items

for different cures; including fruit tree parts. Many fruit tree parts are used to produce medicines– example tamarind pulp is common ingredient in cardiac and blood sugar reducing medicines.

Homeopathy system has many medicines made out of plants, and some out of fruit trees and its parts or fruits.

Even allopathic now is exploring many plants extracts as medicines. This includes fruit trees and fruits too.

11. **As shades:** Many fruit trees are huge trees and if planted on the road sides and foot paths, provide cover and shade for rest. Most of the fruit trees are perennial i.e. they remain green and shady throughout the year.

12. **Maintain & Enhance Biodiversity:** Fruits are eaten by birds and animals. Growing of the fruit trees will also increase the population of birds and animals – making a bountiful nature – a beautiful diverse planet earth to live on.

13. **Arrest Soil Erosion:** Just like any tree, fruit trees also hold the soil and not allow the soil to get eroded during rain or erosion due to wind.

14. **Wasteland Conversion to Bio-active Soil:** If tree is grown on wasteland, falling of tree leaves, fruits and seeds and roots of the tree convert the wasteland to bio-active soil around the tree.

15. **Alternative Energy Source:** Seeds of many fruits are used to extract oil and waste. Both of these two are used as alternative energy source.

16. **Creation of Pleasant Environment:** The greenery created by trees is very pleasant to eyes and that is true for fruit trees too.

17. **Pollution Reduction and Control:** Trees absorb many pollutants and make air cleaner in the localized area. Also plantation of trees close enough to each other for the foliage to make a green wall, physically stops pollution coming inside the surrounded area to a great extent.

18. **Production of Syrup, Squash, Jelly, Jam, Pickles, Morabbas, Chutneys and Chips:** Raw and ripe fruits are used for making various types of tasty items to go as snacks, drinks or food supplements etc.

19. **Seeds and seed oils are used in many Industrial Applications:** Tamarind Seed Kernel Powder is a major industrial product used in textile, paper, jute, food, adhesive, plywood and tanning industries. Coconut waste is used in coir industry.

20. **To rid the cities of monkey menace:** The forest department is experimenting by making a fruit plantation nearby Guwahati to rid/reduce the menace of monkeys in the Guwahati city. Monkeys will move out of the cities to the forests having good supply of fruits as food. Preserving and not reducing the biodiversity is necessary for the humans' survival too.

21. **More Rainfall:** Trees do help in making and attracting rain clouds. Planting fruit trees which grow tall and big will help in enhancing rain fall and make these areas more productive and hospitable.

22. **Long Life with productivity:** Grains need to be sown and harvested every year. Fruit trees are planted and then fruits become available for many years to come with minimal or some care and investment in watering and manures.

Some fruit trees give fruits for 50 years or more – many generations of a family eating fruits from the same tree. Also the land below such trees or plantations are used for cattle grazing (example coconut plantations) or other fruits/grains depending upon the planning of the plantations. Poultry culture also is feasible.

The next three tables give the long life fruit trees (20 years or more), medium life fruit trees (5-20 years) and short life fruit trees (less than 5 years). Most of the fruit trees fall into long or medium life range.

TAble 12: Long Life Fruit Trees (20 years and more)

Fruit	*Life of Tree (years)*	*Time to Fruit (years)*	*Fruit Production per tree each year (kg.)*	*Uses besides eating the fruit §§*
Coconut	50 to 120	2 to 8	10 to 100 nos.	Oil, Copra, Drinks, Fuel, Raw Material for Coir Industry, Brake Linings, Activated Carbon.
Jack Fruit	200	4 to 8	85 to 175	Plant Protenase, Bio-hydrogen, and Plantation for pineapple.
Lichi	50 to 60	5	50 to 120	
Mango	50 to 300	3 to 5	10 to 2000	Mango Oil, Timber
Jamun	70 to 100	5 to 10	50 to 100	The seed is used in various healing systems for curing digestive ailments. The leaves and bark are used for controlling blood pressure and gingivitis. Vinegar and wine is also made.
Apple	60+	3 to 8	40 - 200	Medicinal value- a glucose in small crystals is obtainable from the bark and root inducing artificial diabetes in animals and being researched for human use, in preparation of an ointment for rough skin, bark in decoction for intermittent and bilious fevers. Cooked apples make a good local application for some throat infection. Aesthetic landscaping.

Date Palm	150	4 to 7	80 to 120	Date seeds are soaked and ground up for animal feed. Seeds oil is suitable for use in soap and cosmetics. In preparation of oxalic acid. Seeds are burned to make charcoal for silver smiths. Seeds are used as coffee type of drink. Stripped fruit clusters are used as brooms. Leaves are used for making huts, mats, screens, baskets, fans, insulating boards, rope, coarse clothes, and large hats. Wood is used as fuel. Many medicinal uses too.
Almond	20 to 50	3 to 4	5 + (900–5000 kg/ha)	Almond Oil. Leaves & bark have medicinal value. Gum for book binding etc.
Mahua	60	8 to 15	20 to 200	In production of oil, alcohol. Flowers are edible. Seed cakes after oil extraction as fertilizers. Medicinal uses
Tamarind	200	10 to 14	150 to 225	Medicinal use for intestine ailments, skin infections, Cardiac and blood sugar. Tamarind seed kernel powder (TKP) used in textile, food processing, paper, jute, adhesive, plywood and tanning industries.
Aonla	50 to 60	6 to 8	100 to 150	Dried fruits in medicines of Ayurvedic and Unani systems. Fruit is ingredient in Chayanprash-an Ayurvedic tonic. Fruit is also used for making ink, ordinary dyes, hair dyes, and shampoos and in

				tanning industry.. Wood is used for making agricultural implements, firewood. Hindu worship.
Cashew Nut	30	3	48	The cashew nut shell liquid (CNSL) is mostly composed of anacardic acid-used against tooth abscesses due to their lethality to gram positive bacteria. Bark and seeds in many other medicines. Anacardic acid is also used in chemical industry in manufacture of resins, coatings, frictional materials. To make alcohol-fenny. Shell oil as conditioners & shampoos.
Orange	30 to 40	2 to 3	100 to 290 nos.	Orange peel is used in gingerbread. Many medicinal uses for weight loss, heart ailments. Orange flower's water in culinary preparations. As ornamental tree.
Pomegra-nate	200 (25-30)	2 to 3	136 (60-80 fruits)	Each part of the tree is used for medicinal values.
Guava	20 to 30	2 to 3	100	Useful in Constipation
Safau	50 to 100	4 to 5	220 to 335	Oil for cosmetic and industrial use.
Drumstick (Moringa) (Saijan)	20 +	2 to 3	50 - 70 (20-42 ton/ha)	Fruit, Leaves, Flowers as vegetables. Leaves powdered as micronutrient for treating diseases, Leaves of Exceptional Nutrition Value. Seeds as medicines. All parts of tree of medicinal value Extraction of edible oil, seed

				cake after extraction of oil as fertilizer. Sap for making blue dye. Trees as fences. Leaves are also used for making candy, bio-fuel, and moringa oil. Powdered leaves for purifying water. Seed oil for machinery. Coarse fiber of bark for mats/paper.
Badahal (Lakoocha)	30+	5	80	Edible fruit pulp as tonic for liver, bark for skin ailments. Raw fruits for pickles and chutney. Timber as good as teak. Leaves as animal feed. Wood and roots for making colour dye,
Walnut	200	3 to 15	3-6 ton/ha	Timber. Shells to clean soft metals, fiberglass, plastics. Shells in oil well drilling, paint thickener, explosives, Husk to produce dye. Medicinal use.
Bread Fruit	50	5	150-200 (16-32 ton/ha)	Wood is termite proof. Also used in making paper and screens for interior partition. Fruit is of medicinal value for lowering blood pressure and asthma. Latex to catch birds.
Woodapple (Kaitha or Kathbel)	50+	15	250-1000 (225+ fruits)	Leaves and seed -oils. Medicinal - antiscorbic. Many more medicinal uses - liver and cardiac tonic, sore throat, diseases of gums, cancer, piles. A mixture of the ripe pulp of

				the fruit, cardamom, honey, and cumin seeds used for toning up sagging breasts. Powder of the leaves is used in treating spermatorrhea, or involuntary ejaculation, premature ejaculation and functional impotency etc.
C. apple /Sugar Apple (Sharifa) (Sitaphal)	25+	2-3	4-23 (20-50 fruits)	Leaves, bark of medicinal value. Bark used to produce dye, ink, tattoos, source of hydrogen cyanide. Seed oil as bio-diesel.
Avacado	30+		400-2000 fruits)	Ornamental plant. Avocado oil is edible oil used for cooking and considered equivalent to olive oil. The oil is also used for lubrication and in cosmetics.
Durien	80 to 150	5-21	40 - 50 fruits(6-7 tons/ha)	Medicinal uses
Dragon	20	2 - 3	5 - 6 tons/ha	Ornamental plant, Medicinal Uses.
Mulberry (Sahatoot)	200	3 - 4	abundant	The fruits and leaves are sold as nutritional supplements. To grow silkworm. Food colorants; fabric tanning. Medicinal properties. Tree bark for making paper. Wood for making furniture.
Rambutan		4-7	150	Roots bark, and leave have uses in various medicines and in production of dyes. Seed oil is used in making soaps and candles.

Jujube	20+	2 to 5	50 - 200	Wood for timber and fuel. Tree for fencing. Leaves as fodder. Tanning industry. In lac/shellac production.
Fig	35	1 to 3	140(180-360 fruits)	Medicinal use for constipation, bronchitis. Latex is applied on corns and warts to get rid of the same.
Pear	50	2-3	18 - 25	Wood is preferred material for wood-wind instruments and furniture, wood carving, firewood. Fruits have medicinal value for colitis, gallbladder disorders, arthritis, gout and in lowering of blood pressure, and cholesterol.
Apricot	20	2-3	10-55	Showpiece in landscape. Tree as a housewarming or wedding gift.
Plum	20 to 30	5	9+	In making of alcoholic drink. Fruit has medicinal value.
Cherry	35+	2-3	9 - 20	Diuretic: better kidney function, obesity, dropsy, renal inadequacy. Anti-rheumatic, improves circulatory system, as cardio-tonic. Also in skin diseases. Wood is used in fernery and joining. Leaves and blossoms are edible.
Bael	25+	(5 - 8)	100 - 150 fruits (18-20 tons/ha)	Use in religious rituals. Medicinal uses: anti-bilious, anti- parasitic, aphrodisiac, aromatic, alterative, astringent, digestive, stomachic, stimulant, tonic and laxative properties.

Table 13: Medium Life Fruit Trees (5-20 years)

Fruit	*Life of Tree (years)*	*Time To Fruit (years)*	*Fruit Production per Tree each year (kg.)*	*Uses besides eating the fruit §§*
Karonda	10+3	3	3 - 5	Hedge plant, pickles
Necterinee	15 to 20	3	5 - 10 (10 -37 ton/ha)	Tree as gift
Sapota/ Chiku	13 to 20+	3 - 4	150 (2500-3000) fruits (15-20 tons/ha)	Latex from stem as base material in chewing gum
Guava	12 to 20	2 - 3	100	Useful in constipation
Ber	15 to 20	1 to 8	80 to 200	Leaves as animal fodder. Durable timber, firewood. Many medicinal uses.
Peaches	15 to 20	2 - 3	3 to 20	
Mousambi	15 to 20	5 to 7	300 to 1000 nos.	Blood purifier. Full of vitamin C.
Cardo-mum	15 to 20 to 40+	1 - 2	7 - 22 ton/ha	Oil. Culinary herb. Medicinal herb. Aromatic herb.
Lemon/ Lime	12 to 20	3 - 4	1000 to 5000 nos.	Vitamin C source
Phalsa	10+	1 to 2	7 - 10 ton/ha	Ornamental, medicinal (heart and blood disorders, fever, constipation)
Star Fruit/ Karambola	115+	1-4	80	Medicinal value

TAble 14: Short Life Fruit Trees (Up to 5 years)

Fruit	*Life of Tree (years)*	*Time to fruit (months)*	*Fruit Production per tree each year (kg.)*	*Uses besides eating the fruit §§*
Papaya	2 to 3.5	9 to 12	40 to 75 30 - 45 fruits (65 - 75 ton /ha)	Un-ripe fruit as vegetable. Black seeds are ground and used as substitute to black pepper. Young leaves are cooked like spinach. Marketed in tablet form to remedy digestive problems. Other medicinal uses as contraceptive, juice in treatment of lever, cancer. Papaya seed as anti-bacterial. Latex of un-ripe fruit is used for meat tendering and to provide shrink resistance to wool.
Banana	1 to 2	8 to 12	15 - 60 (40 - 52 tons/ha)	In Indian festivals. The skin of the fruit is used in dyeing. The sap as marking ink. Flowers, central portion of stem, shoot and buds of young plants, unripe fruit are used as vegetables. Leaves are used as plates and wrapping material. All parts are used as medicines too.
Water melon	6 months	2 to 5	25 - 85 ton /ha	Seeds are used in naturopathy as diuretic- to normalize and improve kidney function.
Muskmelon	1	2 to 5	45 ton/ha	
Straberry	3	2	20 - 50 ton /ha	As borders/hedge

(§§ Disclaimer: Information provided in the Table Nos. 12, 13, and 14 is of general nature. The information is not given as medical advice nor it is intended to propose or offer to propose a cure for any disease or condition. Before starting use for any medical treatment, please consult your physician.)

The three tables (Table 12, 13 and 14) are presented to clearly show the followings:

- Most of the fruit trees are having long life and once these trees mature, the fruits are produced for very many years to come.
- The yield or production rate of fruit trees is very high (of course with some care).
- There are plenty of other uses of these trees. Also
  - (a) Though data has not been worked out here, but it is obvious that since trees grow vertical high, with less land, more food is being grown. Fruit trees are like high rise buildings. More population lives per square foot of land for high rise buildings; same way more fruits are produced per square foot of land.
  - (b) There are fruit trees for all type of climates and all types of soil/land. More versatility for food production compared to grains. Even barren lands could be utilized for fruit production.

The information and discussion lead to the following:

"Fruit Tree Plantations and Fruits are big business. Both are absolutely necessary for all to have food and good health; and to keep mother earth a hospitable place to own a house and pleasant living place."

Following large scale programmes will be helpful:

(a) Large tracts of railway land besides railway tracks to be planted with long and medium life fruit trees.

(b) Every railway station to have fruit trees, trees which grow big and provide shades and beauty.

(c) A machine and process to be developed for making one meter diameter and one meter depth pit even in rocky areas, even in rocks. Possible machine, process may use drilling or explosive. This machine and process are to be produced and distributed on mass scale. The pits are to be used for planting fruit trees.

(d) Mechanization of tree plantation process, earth with manure, watering etc. Special purpose equipments and vehicles need to be developed for mechanization of plantation processes. Baby plants raised in leaves powder formed pots will be great help. A vehicle needs to be developed for carrying water; may be just like a snake which climbs and holds stable on all type of terrains.

(e) Plantation and raising of fruit trees to be equated to producing and raising of children. Every man and woman must plant a fruit tree (preferably long life ones) in the name of his father, one in the name of the mother, and one each for each child. Such social changes in thinking will bear fruits quickly for the nation.

(f) Hilly and rocky and arid areas to be encouraged to raise fruits and its plantation. Technical inputs are to be provided free. Rewards, subsidies will go long way to help every citizen with good nourishing food.

(g) Cutting a tree is already a punishable offense. Cutting a fruit tree of long life variety is to be made non-bailable offence.

(h) Fruit preservation and equipments needed for the same to be mass produced and distributed.

(i) Fruits distribution to be supplemented on a wide scale by government owned fruit shops to keep the prices low/ affordable to all – poorest of the poor; and to avoid wastage since private commercial profit greed will waste instead of sale.

(j) Fruits exports to be banned. How a country like India, having so many hungry people or on meager food, exports agricultural products including fruits to other countries? In 2008 data for exports of fruits is given below.

- Total agricultural exports from India in 2007-08 = Rs. 77 769 crore
- Agricultural export of India per citizen = Rs. 650
- Total production of fruits in India = 32 million metric ton
- Fruit production in India per citizen = 27 kg.

Does every citizen in India get on an average 27 kg. of fruits annually?

- Total production of vegetables in India = 71 million metric ton
- Vegetables production in India per citizen = 59 kg.

Does every citizen in India get on an average 59 kg. of vegetables annually?

Table 15: Fruit Exports

Fruit	*India's Export 2007-08*		***Rate/kg. Rs.***
	(kg)	*Rs. Crore*	
Mango	54 350 000	127.42	**23.44**
Banana	16 662 544	26.07	**15.65**
Lichi	161 522	0.63	**39.00**
Apple	32 655 268	33.31	**10.20**
Orange	29 261 300	27.26	**9.30**
Papaya	10 879 728	11.23	**10.30**
Pine Apple	4 194 993	3.39	**8.08**
Grapes	96 963 000	317.82	**32.78**
Lemon	16 222 730	15.49	**9.60**
Pomegranate	35 175 172	91.19	**26.00**
Sapota	2 150 835	5.03	**23.39**

In India, we never get now the above mentioned fruits at the above mentioned prices. We were not getting that at these prices even in the year 2008. Over the above low prices, there is subsidy for the exports of most of the above items. *India is feeding the citizens of other nations and also subsidizing their intake of fruits. India is making the citizens of other nations healthy when the children in India are not even getting proper meals. It could be the greatest irony for any nation.*

Same thing is true for vegetables too. India exported in 2007-08, 1 008 606 metric tons of onions at a revenue of 1035.78 crore. This works out to Rs. 10.27 per Kg rate. In nutrition value, onion is considered next to eggs and even that the poor in India can not afford now at Rs. 20 / kg rate.

- Total exports of fruits and vegetables (2008-2009): = Rs. 4399 crore

  For modern India the above sums are small towards foreign exchange earnings. Why export agricultural produce? Why export fruits and vegetables? And that too the export is made with very heavy export subsidies and benefits.

- India produces :

  41% of world mangoes

  23% of world bananas

  24% of world cashew nuts

  36% of world green peas

  10% of world onions

With population of only 18% of world population; why mangoes, bananas, cashew nuts and green peas have to be so expensive inside India and so cheap in the other countries like America and Europe and Canada?

Why onions have to be exported?

India should earn foreign exchange by exporting

manufactured engineering goods and not by exporting onions.

- India's onion export (2007-2008):

  =1 008 606 metric tons.

In 2008-09, the onions export touched over 18 lakh metric tons.

Encouraging exports of fruits (and also vegetables and grains) is a malodorous and irresponsible practice towards citizens. It must be stopped.

It will be consequential to above decision of stopping fruit and vegetables exports; to stop all subsidies and assistance on fruit and vegetable export purposes. At present government is giving following financial assistance in this regard.

Table 16: Financial Assistance for development of exports of fruits and vegetables

Scheme for:	*Financial Assistance*
• Market Development	100%
• Infrastructure development	25% to 100%
• Vishesh Krisi Up Yojana - duty credit scrip + duty credit for increase in exports	5% of FOB +15% of FOB
• Weightage on FOB or NFE for export of fruits & vegetables	200%
• Vishesh Krishi And Gram Udyog Yojana (VKGUY)	2.5%
- Additional duty free scrip	
• DEPB Scheme - Interest Subsidy	Interest @ 6%
• Income Tax exemption under section 10 B for 100% EOU	Full
• Refund of service tax on services linked to export.	—
• Enhanced incentive under focus product scheme	2.5%

There are many other benefits by central and state governments on export of agricultural items. That is the reason the exports of fruits and vegetables grew by 50% from 2007-08 to 2008-09 in one year. Export of fruits and vegetables during 2007-08 was Rs.2924 crore and it grew to Rs. 4399 crore during 2008-09.

How to make fruits available to everybody at an affordable price?

(a) By making it volume based enterprise; with higher volume of the activity i.e. with more quantities of fruits involved in each activity connected with fruits availability to the population; costs will be distributed on more quantity and hence the price of fruits per kg will be lower.

Also productivity of plantations is to be increased by research, dissemination of information regarding care of plantations by specific manure and watering etc. Present average productivity figures for India are given below.

Government has research institutions specifically for some of the fruits like grapes, pomegranate and so on. However there must be specific research institutes for each type of fruits in every state of India for wider research in different climatic conditions and for spreading awareness regarding care to be taken for increasing productivity without sacrificing edibility.

Table 17: Productivity - Fruit Plantations in India

Fruit	*Average Productivity (MT/Ha)*
Mango	7.8
Citrus	10.1
Banana	28.0
Apple	7.0

Guava	11.05
Sapota	10.8
Pineapple	14.7
Papaya	31.6
Lichi	8.8
Grapes	24.0

(b) The Government subsidy to fruit growers and producers and in the distribution system: It is better to subsidize to maintain good health of its citizens instead of subsidy on health care of its citizens. And also availability of food to all its citizens is governments major and most critical of all its responsibilities.

(c) The Government to fix maximum retail price for each fruit; not in a communist way, but on a proactive enterprise basis.

(d) Land belongs to nobody. Barren land belongs more so to nobody. If any individual, society or organization wish to plant, nurture and maintain long life fruit trees on such barren lands; should be given free by governments and of course with strict monitoring and control on the fruit tree plantation process and maintenance. This will be the right step to reduce the cost and in turn price of fruits to the citizens.

(e) Just like bus stands are built by the road authorities, municipal corporations; covered space for fruit stalls to be built by the same authorities and it must be made as part of integrated road and city development programs/ rural road development programs/village development programs .It should be free for fruit retailers to come at such places and sell fruits. Maximum retail prices to be permanently displayed and retailers using the space must be forced to sell at the prices indicated. This will need enforcement by explanations, persuasion, police and of course ultimately by the consumers.

(f) Fruits tend to get spoiled fast. All efforts and resource generation are required for consumption before spoiling; or delay in the process of spoiling is important. But still there will be wastage and there has to be methodologies to use such spoiled fruits for (i) new plants generation. (ii) manufacture of fruit tree manures. For example spoiled Jamuns could be used for generation of new Jamun plants for further plantation. And also if manure is made out of the spoiled jamuns, manure will have all the ingredients required by the Jamun fruit trees to produce Jamuns and hence will be the best manure for a grown up Jamun tree.

(g) Fruits to be made part of the mid day meal programme for children in schools. This will bring volume in the fruits production and distribution process. And primarily it will improve our future generations' health and will help in reducing drop-out rates. Children love fruits.

(h) There is no point in moving fruits for long distances. It reduces its self life by the time taken for transportation and also increases costs. Local consumption should be encouraged and transportation to long distances to be discouraged. Fixing of maximum retail price for each type of fruit will help in discouraging transportation to long distance destinations and encourage local retail to meet the price.

(i) Bulk transportation of fruits to short and medium distances to be made free by rail. This will improve distribution and reduce wastage. Maybe each train has one or two specially designed cool fruit bogies attached for such transportation.

(j) Prohibit exports of fruits and vegetables for the next 20 years.

Summary

- *The Governments, communities, individuals must sincerely start planting fruit trees on each piece of vacant land inside the nation. This has the best potential to solve food and nourishment issues and global warming in the long range.*

- *Exports of fruits (also vegetables and grains or any food items) to stop immediately for ever.*
- *Creation of ponds, lakes and canals at massive scale both in terms of size and numbers to be started all over India especially on barren lands and rocky hills.*

To banish food shortage and to reduce requirement of healthcare resources in future, it is imperative to plant fruit trees. Every man must plant minimum 5 fruit trees, one each for 2 parents, one each for 2 children and one for spouse.

INDEX

Adulteration, 199
Aeroplanes, Transport, 203
agricultural subsidy, 144
Agriculture, 13
Ahmednagar, 83
Aluminium, 45
Ambanis, 198
America, 63, 73, 86, 233
American, 25
Antarctica Bases, 143, 203
Antyodaya, 10
Arabic, 126
Arthasashtra, 57
Artificial Lakes, 114
Atharvaveda, 63
atoms, 44
Australia, 63
Australian, 60

Bacon, Francis, 33
Bali, 28
Banks, Deposits made in foreign, 58
Barren land, 108, 202
Barter system, 40, 65
Basmati rice, 143
Battle Tanks, 203
Below Poverty Line (BPL), 10
households, 209
Bharatnatyam, 165
Bihar, 102, 208
Bihu, 165
Bio-Diversity, 202, 220
Parks, 119
Bio-active Soil, 220
Bio-Manure, 219
Birlas, 198
Bonds, 33
Brahmaputra, 117
Britain, 63
British farmer, 17
British rule, 125
Bt Brinjal, 213
Bureau of Indian Standards (BIS), 169

Manipuri, 165
Manned Moon Centers, 203
Manusmiriti, 171, 176
Marx, Karl, 54
Maximum Salary Norm, 196
Meat, 84
  Encouragement to eat, 80
Median Income, Average versus, 206
Mercantilism, 56
Middle class, 16
Middle Schools, 202
MIG, 21
Milk, 144, 200
  adulteration, 99
  producer, 145
Ministry of Food Availabilty, 214
Ministry of Food Security, 214
Missile, Nuclear powered, 204
Missiles, 202
Mlesksha,award for foreigners, 28
Monarchy democracy, 171
Monetary policy, 140, 141, 142, 150, 151
Money, 30, 32, 33, 41
Monkey, 221
Moon, manned base on the, 134
Mother's day, 25
Mumbai, 180

Nation, Population of a, 47
National Development Index (NDI) 211
National Institute of Hyderabad, 97
National Planning Process, 34
National Poverty, 25
National Wealth, 57
National Wealth, Money is not, 31
Natural resources, 46
New York, 195
North Korea,131
Nuclear Engines, 204
Nuclear Submarines, 203

Odissi, 165, 165
Onions, 200
Orange, 192

Pakistan, 80, 125
PAN Card,175
Person, Evita, Argentinean politician, 19
Physical Poverty, 21, 23
Planning, 108
Pollution, 220
Pomegranate, 192
Population, 59
Potatoes, 200
Poultry, 80
Pounds, 73
Poverty, 20
  Removal of, 9, 77
  Total Removal, 182
Power Industry, 219
Primary Schools, 202
Private enterprises, 140
Producers, subsidy to fuit growers and, 236
Protestant countries, 52
Public Distribution System, 103
Pulses, 78
  shortage of, 79
Pune, 179
Punjab, 117
Purchasing Power Parity (PPP), 26, 27, 66

R&D, 132
  Projects, 133, 203
Races, brown, yellow and black, 28
Railway Stations, 203

Rajasthan, 117
Red Indians, 125
Research Institutes, 203
Reusable Space Shuttle, 203
Rice, 78, 200
Right to Information Act, (2005) 174
River Banks, 202
  Construction of, 112
Rivers, Connect the, 115
Rivers, Dredging of, 112, 202
Robot soldiers, 204
Roman empire, 52
Russia, 6, 118, 131
Russian, 126

Sangh Rajya (centralized akin to Communism), 56
Satellites, 204
Satellites, Development of, 134
Sea Bases (Mineral Mining Centers), 203
Sea Bottom Military Bases, 204
Seeds, 221
SEZ, 214
Shares, 33
Ships, 203
Shiva, dance of, 122
Sikkim, 85
Singapore, 56
Small car, 147
Smith, Adam, 54
Social Poverty, 23
Socialism, 56, 171
Soil Erosion, 220
South Africa, 73
South Korea,72
Soviet Union, 125
Space Satellites, 113, 202
Space Technology, 131
Spanish, 126
Spritual wealth, 53
Standardization, 166
  Benefits of, 161
  Risks of, 165
Stem cells, 124, 135
Stock market, 194
Subsidies, Central Government, 154
Subsidies, government direct or indirect, 195
Subsidy, 39
Sugriv, 28
Super computers, 203, 204

Taiwan, 67
Taj Mahal, 111
Tatas, 198
Technology, Standardization, 164
The Times of India, 137
Theory of Population, 60
Townships, 202
Toyota car, 60
Trees, Advantage of Fruit, 217
Trees, Planting fruit, 221
Trees, medium, and short life fruit, 192

U.N., official languages of, 126
Udyogi, mindset of being, 178
Udyogi Mindset, 183
UK, 48, 130
Underground Shelters (Nuclear Protection), 203
United Kingdom, 210
United Nations, 126
United Nations Security Council, 127
United States of America, 43
UP, 208
Uranium, 44

USA, 16, 17, 48, 98, 118, 130, 151, 210
airport in, 111
Uttarakhand, 85

Vajpayee, 137
Valentine's Day, 24
Vasco de Gama, 17
Vegetables, exports of fruits and, 235
Vegetables, increasing production of, 87
Vindhyas, 83
Vocational Education, 153
Vocational Technical Training Centers, 154

Water, 45
Canals, 113, 202
Wealth of Nations, 54
Wealth, Creating National, 201
Wealth, Indian Citizens, 52
Wealth, Methods of Creation of, 52
Wealth, Money is not, 63
Wealth, creating national, 186, 191
Weatlh, TV is not an essential, 54
Wealth, types of, 77
West Bengal, 102, 208
West UP, 117
Wheat, 78, 200
Whites, 28
World Bank, 208